NEVIS
QUEEN OF THE CARIBBEAN

BY DEBORAH LELLOUCH

Contributing Writers:
DAPHNE HOBSON
VINCENT HUBBARD

PHOTOGRAPHS BY

JERÔME DE BAECQUE

and

DEBORAH LELLOUCH

Photographer photographed

ISBN 976-8173-46-7 (hdc)

Pre-press by:
COT CARIBBEAN GRAPHICS
CHRIST CHURCH, BARBADOS

Printed by:
KINGSLEY PRINT & DESIGN LTD.
SURREY, ENGLAND

P.O. BOX 640, UPPER GOVERNMENT ROAD
CHARLESTOWN, NEVIS, WEST INDIES

CONTENTS

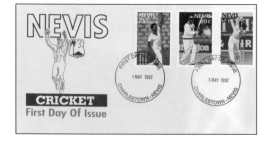

INTRODUCTION

This book is dedicated to those who have loved Nevis from birth . . . and to those who will experience the joy of discovering an island unlike any other.

Who, better, to describe the beauties, the uniqueness of their homeland, than our native sons and daughters, the Staff of the Ministry of Tourism, whose pride and mission it is to lure and welcome you to Nevis.

Here, they share with enthusiasm their personal "favourites" to whet your appetite for what is to come:

VANESSA evokes with fondness her fun-filled childhood memories of pick-up cricket games played in a field after school, of Summer days spent traipsing through the lush-green scented pastures with village playmates in search of the seasonal fruit our climate provides in abundance: juicy mangoes, sugar apples, soursops, cashew-nuts and tamarinds. A mother herself, now, she delights in sharing these pastimes with her young children, knowing that they can enjoy the same sense of freedom and discovery today.

LAUREN, who is away on study-leave, longs for the exhilarating breeze she loves to "drink in" like a tonic at dawn from a hilltop overlooking the ocean. In the midst of city smells and pollution, she dreams of air that is pure and sweet and refreshing — with just a tang of the sea.

CHARMAINE succumbs to the charm of natural smiling faces all about us. She teasingly suggests: "If you don't know us, you'll probably think we're flirting!" And what a sense of security comes from knowing everyone is concerned about everyone else. "Some say it's a place where everybody's business is yours; but isn't it a unique way of protecting our island and our people?"

ANGELIQUE concurs that Nevisian warmth and friendliness make everyone feel welcome here. Her favourite image, and one that always fills her with awe, is the view one has from every angle of majestic Nevis Peak, when clouds form a halo over the summit, just as Christopher Columbus sighted our island when he named her "Nuestra Señora de las Nieves" (Our Lady of the Snows).

DEVON is a "serious" lover of nature, and knows more backroads and hidden mountain paths than he is willing to reveal. Suffice it to say that one is safe to venture anywhere, and discovery is just around the bend, whether one follows the well-marked Upper Round Road, a Nature Hike with one of our expert guides, a search for medicinal plants, a Dive Trip to explore the flora and fauna around our coastline, or simply a lovers' stroll along a pristine beach at sunset.

ELMEADER projects, in her mind's eye, an image of what she loves best about Nevis: "Give me the beauty of nature !!Splashed!! with warm and friendly faces." And, what more could one ask? The place and the people; that's Nevis in a nutshell.

3

YVETTE calls Nevis "the ideal hideaway" where you forget dates and diaries and are lured to consume the scenic beauty around you. She especially enjoys forays into Nevis' rich history. Abandoned sugar mills, once-lavish estates, churches with their evocative tombstones, and pre-Columbian sites and relics dot our island, and take us on an imaginary trip to centuries past. How was life then? We look for quiet signs and clues, and long to talk with our ancestors. The high-speed communication of the cyber-world seems far, far away.

DEBORAH can think of "nowhere on earth" she would rather be than her cool and airy West Indian home, nestled on three acres of gently-rolling land, dominated by verdant Nevis Peak. Open ceilings, lattice arches and fine fretwork attest to the craftsmanship of years gone by. Well-worn floors echo the patter of forgotten footsteps. Familiar creaks and sighs, like voices from the past, tell of those who have loved and cared for her. Past, present and future cohabit in perfect harmony, giving a sense of well-being and timelessness to all who enter in. Our lovely historic Plantation Inns will make you feel you're "at home" in Nevis, too.

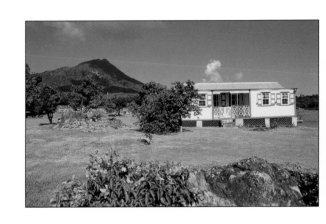

NATACHA looks forward every year to the festive period of Culturama, a week-long celebration overlapping July and August, featuring Calypso Contests, Miss Culture Queen Pageant, Jammin', Food Fairs, Masquerades and Plays, and a Grand Parade Finale . . . and well she might! Our beautiful and talented colleague not only survived the spirited competition, but went on to win the title "Miss Culture Queen" in 1998, and represented the Island of Nevis on many occasions at home and abroad. Her work in the Tourism Sector is a natural outcome of her ability to project our best image.

TYRONE agrees that Culturama is his favourite time of the year, too. Always a touch of nostalgia as old friends return from all corners of the globe to celebrate just as in the "good old days", knowing that in Nevis they can go anywhere, anytime, without being harassed or molested in any way. He asks, rhetorically: "How many places like this are left?"

JEANNETTE enjoys the pastoral peacefulness which complements the beauty of our natural environment. Where else can you still see old men going to their land on donkeys? Or young boys catching a donkey colt and riding him just for sport? "Some might say Nevis lives in the past; I say Nevis is traditional and unspoilt!"

CHARLES cites the qualities which give Nevisians such a singular character: resiliency, warmth, genuine hospitality and friendliness, concern and respect for all individuals, bonding together so as not to leave anyone out of daily life and enterprise. Inclusion and encouragement are the goals of an integrated society, from the deaf-mute craftsman to the Special Olympian. Everyone has a place.

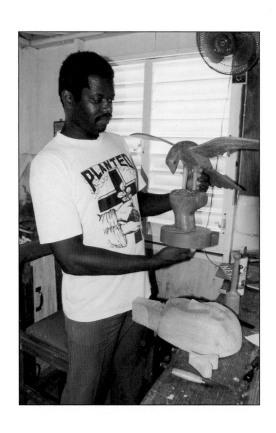

MALCOLM, like the legendary Marcel Proust and his "madeleines", cherishes culinary memories from earliest childhood of favourite dishes his Mother cooked for the family: traditional saltfish and johnnycakes on Good Friday, fragrant curried mutton for Sunday dinner, spicy barbecued chicken to eat with your fingers, and a pot of rice 'n peas always steaming on the back burner. Her coconut tarts had a way of disappearing even before they reached the table! Along with fondly-remembered tastes and aromas, come warm feelings of times past when a meal was truly an occasion for fellowship and good conversation. Thank goodness, the ladies of Nevis have not lost these family recipes. You, too, can enjoy them in local restaurants and at food fairs.

GEOGRAPHY

LOCATION

The island of Nevis belongs to the Leeward Islands of the West Indies archipelago and is one of a chain of relatively young volcanic islands stretching from Saba to Grenada.

At a latitude of 17°10' and a longitude of 62°35', Nevis is located two miles southeast of St Kitts. A channel called "the Narrows", notorious for its rough seas, separates the two islands. Its bottom is covered with magnificent coral reefs. The perimeter of this small island paradise is bordered by long stretches of sandy beach broken by occasional rocky promontories.

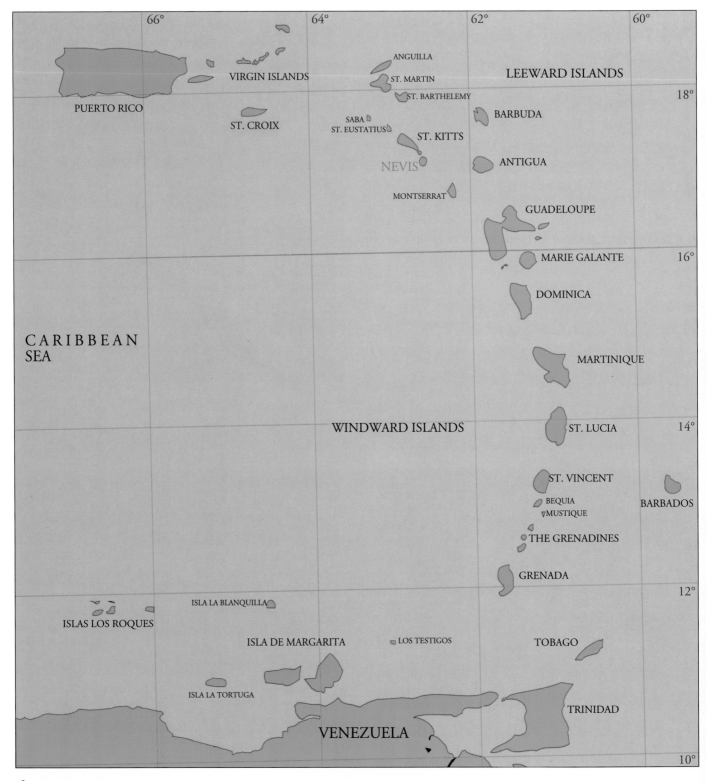

TOPOGRAPHY AND GEOLOGY

The island is dominated by a central volcanic cone, Nevis Peak, whose cloud-crowned summit rises to a height of 3,232 feet (985 meters). The form of the island is nearly circular, covering an area of 36 square miles (92 square kilometers). Windy Hill to the north and Saddle Hill to the south line up with Nevis Peak to form a NNW/SSE watershed. Geologists have identified many types of volcanic and sedimentary rocks which, under the influence of various microclimates, have evolved into a great diversity of soils rich in mineral elements required by plants. Many of these, however, are considered to have little agronomic value due to insufficient drainage and the presence of volcanic boulders which inhibits the development of mechanized agriculture.

CLIMATE

Located 6° south of the Tropic of Cancer, Nevis is characterized by a tropical and maritime climate, strongly influenced by steady Northeasterlies. There is a wide range of microclimates which vary greatly with height, location and orientation.

Tradewinds break against Nevis Peak, creating orogenic cloud formations which rarely dissipate. Annual rainfall averages 46 inches (1,170 millimeters) at sea level. The climate is remarkable, even by Caribbean standards. Sunshine is guaranteed virtually every day of the year. Temperatures average 78° Fahrenheit (25° centigrade) year 'round. There is a constant cooling breeze from the sea, and humidity is very low. There is no rainy season as such, but short and heavy rainshowers occur from July to January. Tropical storm activity is carefully monitored in the region, and advisories are broadcast via the Weather Channel from June through November.

The rocky shoreline at New River

The luxuriant vegetation in the rain-forest

VEGETATION

The present vegetation has evolved as a result of both human activity and climatic conditions. Above an altitude of 1,300 feet (400 meters), Nevis Island is covered with an evergreen tropical forest. Only faint light penetrates the thick, luxuriant leaves, creepers and vines, while the ground is entirely covered with ferns.

Near the summit of Nevis Peak, this exuberant forest tends to disappear and is gradually replaced by gnarled shrubs, moss, and magnificent clusters of orchids.

What is left of the original jungle can be found above Jessups on the northwestern slopes of Nevis Peak, where the high and dense canopy of leaves remains undamaged. Dominant species are mountain cabbage palms (Euterpe globosa) gumlins (Dacryodes excelsa) and burrwood (Slonea truncata).

Below 1,300 feet (400 meters), very little original vegetation is left, as farm land and a golf course occupy most of the remaining surface. A littoral belt of vegetation, resistant to the salty ocean spray, serves a vital function in preventing the erosion of sand and soil.

Salt and fresh water mix in swamps along the coast; mangrove trees grow in these shallow waters, and provide a sanctuary for many species of migrant birds.

Flamboyant (our national tree)

FLORA

The island is a veritable Garden of Eden, of interest to botanists and amateurs alike.

In the wild, or in parks and private gardens, an infinite diversity of tropical flora can be admired all year 'round. Magenta bougainvilleas, pink or white oleanders, variegated hibiscus, vermillion flamboyants, yellow allamandas . . . The air is balmy with the scent of the flowering frangipani trees. In the plains area, Royal palms and coconut trees grow everywhere. Easy-to-reach avocados, bananas, breadfruit, mangos, papayas and citrus fruits are staples of the Nevisian diet.

Hibiscus

Papaya tree

8

Coconut grove at Nelson's Spring

Domesticated donkey

Great white heron

FAUNA

The fauna, typical of the Caribbean, consists of small and innofensive mammals, lizards, birds, and aquatic creatures, many of which arrived on the island aboard seagoing vessels. The Vervet Monkey, playful and gregarious, inhabits the lush forest areas, feeding on mangos and papayas, often stolen from nearby gardens. Some of the best spots for observing "monkey business" are the ghauts leading down from the Golden Rock Estate where, at dawn and dusk, they can be seen in family groups. Frequent visitors to the outdoor restaurants include "sugar birds" and tiny lizards, searching for crumbs and tidbits. Birds come in all colors and sizes, from the green-throated carib to the great white heron. Minute crested hummingbirds drink nectar from deep-throated ginger blossoms. The brown pelican, national symbol and fisherman, *par excellence,* can be seen diving after schools of flying fish near the coast. Farmyard animals are part of the landscape, and of the micro-economy of the island. The sea fauna is rich. Along the shore, crabs, conch, lobsters and nesting sea turtles can be seen by those who enjoy snorkeling. Deep-sea fishing with seasoned professionals offers the opportunity to catch swordfish, wahoo and even sharks. There are no snakes, and the rare insect bites recorded are non-lethal. Nevis, in all its splendor, affords the visitor a rare opportunity to commune with nature.

Red dragonfly

Green lizard

Brown pelican

HISTORY OF NEVIS

By Vincent K. Hubbard,

Author of *Swords, Ships and Sugar: a History of Nevis to 1900*

The first human inhabitants of Nevis were pre-ceramic Indians called Sibonay. They are believed to have come to Nevis around 2,000 years ago from Central America, but the place of their origin is not certain. At any rate, all that remains of them here are a few primitive stone or shell tools. They were followed by Arawak Indians, who came from the Orinoco River Basin in Venezuela. The Carib Indians, who came from the same general area of South America, arrived several hundred years later. There are 22 known Indian sites in Nevis, marked with sherds of pottery, pieces of flint stone, and shell heaps. From time to time human bones are found when erosion exposes them. Archaeologists estimate that, between 500 and 600 A.D., the Indian population of Nevis was anywhere from 1,000 to 5,000.

Nevis and all the Leeward Islands were designated "useless islands" by Spain, which claimed the entire Caribbean from the time of Columbus' second voyage to 1671. Columbus officially claimed Nevis (originally named St. Martin) on 11 November 1493, when he anchored overnight off the west coast of the island. Within 50 years of Columbus' voyage, the name of the island appeared on maps as "Nieves", the Spanish word for snow. The clouds around the mountain peak evidently looked like a snow cap to early sailors.

The Spanish Crown allowed the taking of Carib Indians as slaves, because they were cannibals, but not the Arawaks. It was not then, and is not now clear, what differences there were between the two peoples. The near elimination of the Indian population of both Nevis and the Caribbean by Spanish slave raids, and the spread of European diseases unwittingly carried by them, is one of the most tragic chapters in human history. By 1600, there were only a handful of Indians left in Nevis, if indeed there were any permanent Indian residents here. It was noted by an 18th-Century writer that the remaining Indians were expelled from Nevis, St. Kitts and Antigua in 1640; but, in 1680, a census of Nevis indicated there were a few still working as slaves on Nevis plantations.

A general view of the island from the west side

The earliest written record of a visit to Nevis was in 1603, by Captain Bartholemew Gilbert, of Plymouth, England. He does not mention seeing any Indians here. The purpose of his trip was to harvest *lignum vitae* logs. This wood, no longer found in Nevis, was so heavy it would not float, and so hard termites could not eat it. It was sometimes used for industrial gear wheels in place of iron. Gilbert commented that sea turtles were abundant, and some were so large that a single one fed his 24 men for three days.

In 1607, Captain John Smith and his men stopped for five days in Nevis on their way to found the colony of Virginia in North America. He wrote that he established a carefully-guarded camp in case of Indian attack, and his men encountered an Indian hunting party inland, but both groups ran from each other and there was no confrontation. Smith remarked that Nevis was completely wooded from the edge of the sea to the top of the mountain, and that there was a hot water spring (the Bath Spring) whose waters would cure gunpowder burns and serious skin irritations. A 1608 visitor declared those waters could cure leprosy and coughs as well. This spring still exists on the grounds of the ruins of the Bath Hotel, built in 1778, as the first resort hotel in the Caribbean.

The Bath Spring was famous among early European explorers in the Caribbean, and Nevis became a common stopover, especially for English and Dutch ships passing through the area on their way to North America. Spain claimed all the islands for themselves, and their navy was so powerful that the Caribbean was termed "a Spanish lake" in the 16th and 17th Centuries. Any non-Spanish vessels venturing into it did so at their peril.

In 1620, an incident occurred on the west coast of Nevis in which two Spanish men-of-war, one of 16 and the other of 20 guns, and both disguised to look like Dutch merchant ships, lay in wait for trespassers. A small English merchantman on her way to Virginia, the eight-gun *Margaret and John* of London, stopped at Nevis for fresh water. She carried 109 people on board, mostly migrating families, and six French sailors who had been shipwrecked in Martinique for six months and had lived with the Indians. The Frenchmen warned the English Captain that they had seen two Spanish warships in Martinique earlier, and they believed the vessels anchored in Nevis were the very same ones.

A longboat was sent out to hail the unidentified ships. When the sailors determined the vessels were indeed Spanish, they came about and raced back toward *Margaret and John* at full speed. The warships immediately ran up the Spanish flag and opened fire on the longboat with muskets and swivel cannon. One man reported a ball passed through his jacket and the bottom of the boat, and he plugged up the hole with his handkerchief. *Margaret and John* attempted to escape, but her anchor had fouled on the bottom and could not be raised. Helpless, she was attacked by one Spanish warship which came alongside, fired a broadside into her, and attempted a boarding. After a brutal hand-to-hand fight on the deck, the attackers were driven off. The Spanish Captain was killed leading his men over the rail. Nineteen men were killed on *Margaret and John*, including three of the French sailors, before the anchor cable was cut and she managed to escape.

This small battle was indicative of the ongoing conflicts between European powers which would later engulf Nevis. Literally, the Caribbean would be the anvil for European wars until the mid-19th Century. In 1625, Nevis was unofficially settled by Englishmen coming from St.Kitts. Officially, it was settled in 1628, and the first Governor of Nevis then proceeded to steal the island's first tobacco crop. His career was cut short when Nevis was invaded by the Spanish in 1629, and the tiny settlement was destroyed and the settlers dispersed. Much of the land-clearing - dangerous and difficult work - was being done by indentured Irish Roman Catholic servants who disliked the Protestant English, joined the Spanish invaders, and left Nevis for good.

Commemorative Plaque at Museum of Nevis History

The first European immigrants to the island were usually indentured for a period of three to five years and were, in effect, contract slaves. They would exchange their labor for a term to a person paying their passage across the sea, and these contracts could be bought and sold. Europeans found it difficult to adjust to the heat; their diet was poor, and the resulting death rate was so high that fewer than half of them lived to see the end of their indenture periods. Male indentured servants exceeded female by a three-to-one ratio, and, as a result, there was chronic drunkenness and fighting among them. However, those who finished their indentures were usually able to obtain land and became small farmers.

The first commercial enterprise on Nevis was small farming of cotton, tobacco, indigo, and vegetables. The cultivation of sugar cane and the ability to crystallize it (a secret brought by Dutch traders and Jewish emigrants from Brazil) changed the island completely. By 1642, Nevis was acknowledged to produce the finest sugar in the Caribbean, and its population was estimated to be 10,000, when Virginia had a population of only 8,000. It was noted, in 1727, that one gallon of cane juice from Nevis produced 24 ounces of sugar, when the average in the Caribbean was only 16 ounces per gallon. For a time, Nevis became fabulously rich from sugar.

Sugarmill at work

Sugar production was, however, a labor-intensive process, and European labor became difficult to obtain because of the very high death rate in the Caribbean. At that point, the importation of African slave labor commenced. As with the indentured servants, their death rate was extremely high. It was estimated that about 22% would die on the "middle passage" voyage from Africa to Nevis, and approximately two-fifths of those who survived the trip died becoming "seasoned" to life here. Nevis reached the height of its prosperity in the last quarter of the 17th Century. It was the richest Caribbean island, save Barbados. In 1675, Nevis became the depot for the slave trade for all the Leeward Islands. The average number of slaves passing through Nevis in that era was 6,000 to 11,000 annually. Nevis planters naturally selected the best slaves for themselves, much to the distress of planters on the other islands.

This prosperity was achieved in spite of almost constant warfare and the natural devastations of hurricanes and earthquakes. Several times in the 17th Century, Nevis barely avoided being taken by the French and Dutch. In 1667, France very nearly took all the Leeward Islands from England. St. Kitts, Montserrat and Antigua were captured one by one, and only Nevis, the richest, most populous and best fortified, remained in English hands.

In 1666, a French attack was repelled, and, had a follow-up attack been made with stronger forces, Nevis probably would have been captured. Nearly 5,000 refugees from other islands had fallen back to Nevis, and food and military ordnance were in very short supply.

West Indies Governor Lord Willoughby, in Barbados, realized it was essential to Great Britain that Nevis be held. He gathered a fleet of 17 ships, 1,000 troops, 2,000 muskets, and supplies of food and military ordnance, and sailed to the relief of Nevis. He never made it. On 18 July 1666, a massive hurricane caught his fleet off Guadeloupe. Every single ship was lost, and Lord Willoughby and 1,500 men were drowned. Bodies and wreckage of his ships washed ashore throughout the Leewards. Nevis itself was devastated by the hurricane. The inhabitants had to leave their collapsing houses and throw themselves flat on the ground in open fields to survive. Had the French been able to mount an attack, Nevis undoubtedly would have fallen; but the French islands had been hit by the storm as well, and it was not possible for them to send troops to Nevis for some months.

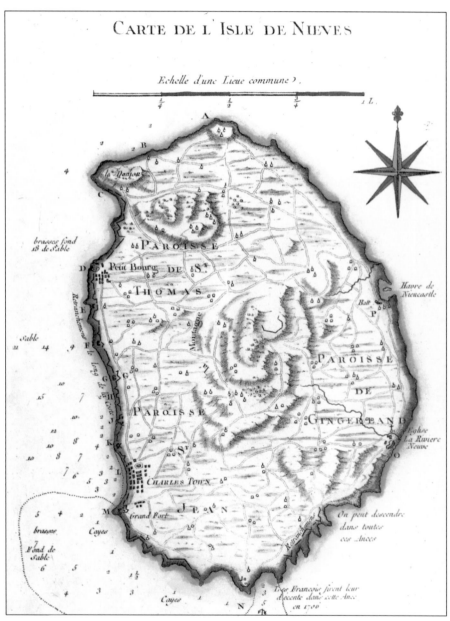

A French map dating from the 18th Century

The French prepared a careful plan for an invasion of Nevis. A combined Franco-Dutch fleet of 30 ships was assembled in Guadeloupe under the overall command of General de la Barre. Sixteen were French men-of-war, ranging in size from 20 to 38 guns, and three were Dutch men-of-war under the command of Admiral de Crynsens, two of 28 guns and one of 38 guns. The remainder of the vessels were supply ships and troop carriers. The Carib Indians were allied with the French as well, and the Indians arrived on the east side of Nevis in a fleet of large war canoes carrying 30 to 40 warriors per vessel. If the French and Dutch landed on the western side of the island, the Caribs would take their shallow draft canoes over the reefs and attack on the eastern side. The militia could not defend both sides of the island at once. It was a very sound plan.

The British, however, had dispatched ten warships carrying desperately-needed supplies to Nevis, under the command of Captain (later Admiral) Sir John Berry, "an expert seaman and a courageous, bold commander". Berry's flagship was the *HMS Coronation*, a powerful 50-gun ship of the line. The Franco-Dutch fleet was detected approaching Nevis, and Berry launched an immediate attack against the larger fleet. "He had the weather gauge in his favor", meaning the wind was astern of his ships. De la Barre was not a naval commander, and could not decide whether to stand and fight Berry or protect his supply ships; and, therefore, he did not meet Berry's attack forcefully, as the Dutch Admiral urged him to do.

The battle raged for four hours. In the thick of the fight, off the southwest coast of Nevis, one of Berry's warships blew up and sank with heavy loss of life. Admiral de Crynsens then moved to engage *Coronation* with all three of his men-of-war, and the battle turned in favor of the combined fleet. However, Berry ordered that a fireship be sent against de Crynsens' vessels, which forced them to bear off before his flagship was heavily damaged, and the tide of battle turned in his favor once again. At last, De la Barre broke off action and withdrew to St. Kitts, giving Berry a victory and ultimately enabling Britain to retain all the Leewards. The Caribs quickly departed following the engagement.

In 1673, the Dutch attacked Nevis with 15 ships and 1,100 men, hoping to land troops and capture the island. During the attack, the Dutch ships received such a pounding from Nevis' shore batteries that onshore observers noted sailors going over the sides with wooden plugs to stop up leaks caused by cannonballs. Not only were the Dutch unable to land troops, they were not even able to take any merchant ships as prizes, although they tried repeatedly.

Fort Charles

The years 1689 and 1690 were devastating for Nevis. During those years, successive epidemics of fever, ague, and bloody flux killed nearly half of the population. Nevis went from being the strongest of the Leewards to the weakest, and a terrible earthquake, in 1690, caused all the brick and stone buildings to "drop of a sudden from top to bottom in perfect ruins". However, in spite of natural and man-made calamities, Nevis continued to grow more and more prosperous.

In 1671, construction of Fort Charles began. In that year the Leeward Islands became a separate colony and wealthy Nevis was its seat. It remained so for over 50 years. The fort was completed within the decade by slave labor and mounted 26 cannon. Combined with nine other batteries on the Leeward side of the island, Nevis was very well protected, and Charlestown was then considered the best fortified harbor in the Caribbean. Even before the fort was finished, the Dutch tested it with an attack. Its guns were continually used against pirate attacks and those of other enemies, usually the French.

In those years, there was a protocol in effect that required a foreign ship entering the harbor to strike its colors. In response, the shore batteries would fire a blank cannon salute. The purpose was to show that the two nations were not at war. If a vessel failed to strike, a shot would be fired from land across her bows as a warning. If she did not then strike, worse would follow. In 1679, a small French merchantman named *La Sara de Rochelle* entered Charlestown harbor and failed to strike her colors. A warning shot was duly fired from Fort Charles. Captain Michel, "the impudent fellow", as the Governor called him, responded by firing a cannon at the British flag flying over the Fort. This action resulted in angry return fire from the fort, which missed its target. Captain Michel bore off to French St. Kitts, but left Nevis' Governor Sir William Stapleton infuriated. Stapleton wrote to England: "It frets me to skin and bones to see such indignities heaped on the King's flag by their very merchantmen."

In 1700, a similar occurrence took place which had more serious and long-lasting consequences. French Admiral de Modene arrived in Charlestown with three powerful ships of the line. His visit was expected, and the nations were at peace, but he failed to strike his colors. As he anchored, a warning shot was fired across his bows from Fort Charles. A longboat was sent from shore to determine why he had not lowered his flag as protocol demanded. Evidently very much offended, de Modene apologized and promised to strike. He further declared that, after the salute was fired from the fort, he would fire a salute to England from his warship's guns as an act of contrition.

The cannon at Fort Charles had been loaded with shot, but it was removed; and, at the appointed time, the fort's guns fired their blank salute. De Modene, however, ordered all the guns of his three vessels to be fully loaded, and, rather than firing a blank salute, his flagship fired a full broadside into the fort and his other two ships fired broadside after broadside into Charlestown. People of every station of life had gathered on the bayfront to witness this military spectacle, and many were killed or wounded by shot. Several English merchantmen, anchored in the harbor, responded by firing at the French warships with their small cannon, but were battered into submission before their guns had any effect. De Modene sailed away leaving much damage in the town and an abiding distrust of the French, by the entire population, which would manifest itself in 1706, when England and France were once again at war.

The war of the Spanish succession began in 1703, and pitted Great Britain and Holland against France and Spain. The results were soon felt in the Caribbean. In February 1706, a French fleet under the command of Admiral Count de Chauvanac attacked Nevis with 24 ships and 1,100 troops. They anchored off Cades Bay and Pinney's Beach on the western side of the island and attempted to land troops. The attack was expected. Four hundred and thirty Nevis militia and 125 British regulars, brought from Antigua under the command of Governor John Johnson, were waiting. Their strong resistance, combined with heavy seas, prevented a French landing for five days, despite repeated attempts. Count de Chauvanac gave up the attempt, but went on to poorly-prepared St. Kitts, captured it in a single day, and spent three days plundering it. Over 600 slaves were taken from St. Kitts and much damage was done.

Fort Charles cannon

Rich Nevis, however, remained the prime target of the French. In March 1706, with their forces increased to 36 ships and 2,100 troops, the French, under the command of Pierre Le Moyne d'Iberville, the founder of Louisiana in North America, approached Nevis a second time. This attack was much better planned. D'Iberville approached from the South, and sailed around the eastern side of the island with the main body of his fleet, but he left six supply vessels anchored off the south side of Nevis. These vessels were ignored by the Nevis land commander, as they were not warships – a great mistake. D'Iberville had secreted himself and 900 troops on board. The main fleet circled the island and anchored off the western beaches at approximately the same place as before. At dawn on Good Friday, the warships opened fire on the shore batteries with a thunderous bombardment. However, this time Governor Johnson and the 125 regulars were in Antigua, and only 430 militia opposed them on the beaches.

Slaves working in the sugar cane fields

D'Iberville, hearing the distant cannon fire, immediately landed his 900 troops unopposed and marched North towards Charlestown. They were soon discovered, but only a handful of militia were available to oppose them. The militia fought bravely, but were quickly overwhelmed in spite of assistance from Fort Charles' cannon. The fort was then taken when d'Iberville's troops forced the landward entrance. When the fort fell, 22 British merchant ships in Charlestown harbor lost their protection, and all were captured. The French troops marched from there into Charlestown, where they plundered and fired the town. The rest of the Nevis militia retreated from the beaches and headed for a mountain redoubt, where they could withstand a siege. D'Iberville's forces pressed them on the retreat, and a battle occurred at Morning Star Plantation where the outnumbered militia were again defeated.

The militia made their way to the redoubt, where they were in a strong defensive position. However, in an "ignominious" surrender, they capitulated the next morning without firing a shot. Nevis had fallen in three days to d'Iberville's well- planned and executed attack, and his troops systematically began to pillage the island. The slaves, however, did not give up. Thirty-four hundred were captured initially and subsequently transported to Martinique, but about 1,000 more, poorly armed and militarily untrained, made their way up Mount Nevis

A windmill in function

and established a defensive position. When French troops advanced to attack, they were driven back, time and again, by "murderous fire". It was written by an English militiaman that the slaves' "brave behavior and defense there shamed what some of their masters did, and they do not shrink to tell us so". The slaves held 18 days until the French left the island, mistakenly believing that a British fleet was approaching. It is likely that Admiral de Modene's action, in 1700, encouraged them to take such a strong stand in 1706.

Angered by the slaves' unexpected resistance, d'Iberville demanded that the planters turn over 1,400 more slaves or pay a tribute of 30 pounds per slave; and, to enforce his demand, he took three leading planters hostage and carried them to Martinique, where they languished in prison until 1715.

Nevis was devastated by this savage attack. In 1704, its sugar production had been 2,965 tons, but it plunged to only 533 tons in 1706. The 1704 figures would not be equalled again for eighty years. The British Parliament voted 100,000 pounds in aid for Nevis, but that was only a tenth of the island's losses. The sad fact was that Nevis would never fully recover, and its economy began a decline which would continue until its almost total failure in the 1920's and 1930's.

Loading of boats

The 18th Century was a difficult one for Nevis. Twenty-six hurricanes would strike the island with devastating results. In 1725 and 1726, starvation threatened because of drought. An incipient slave rebellion was discovered in 1725, but stopped before violence could occur when two of the alleged leaders were captured by the militia and burned alive. The overall population declined and the percentage of Europeans fell from one-quarter of the population to one-tenth during that century. As the fertility of the soil declined from exhaustion and erosion, more slaves were required to manure and prepare the land in order to maintain the same level of sugar production. Sugar prices remained high because of growing demand in Europe, but the cost of production in Nevis increased, and the profit margin for planters narrowed. Slaves frequently suffered from lack of food and the poor nutritional content of food they did receive. Sugar was so valuable that the land available for planting food crops shrank. It was more economical to grow sugar, sell it to Britain, and buy food products in bulk from North America.

This trade system would come to a halt with the American Revolution. Food imports from the 13 rebellious colonies stopped entirely during the war, which lasted from 1776 to 1783. Three to four hundred slaves starved to death in Nevis, and many more were so weakened by malnutrition that they had low resistance to disease and died of natural causes. A Nevis planter wrote to England in 1777, that because of the war, he would "go bankrupt or starve to death, or both". This very nearly came true.

West Indian planters, on the whole, were sympathetic to the North American rebels, and, had they had the power to do so, would probably have joined them. By 1776, the Nevis economy had generally recovered from the 1706 disaster, but she had been left behind in development by the other Leewards, and had become the poorest and least productive of them all. What struck immediate fear into Nevis, was the entry of France on the American side of the war in 1778. Shortly afterward, Spain and Holland followed. British sea power was drawn off to North America, and the Caribbean was wide open to Britain's enemies. Nevis attempted to rebuild its defenses, but lacked the funds to do so effectively.

The first enemy contact was with a 38-vessel warfleet under the command of French Admiral Count d'Estaing, which was blockading Charlestown Harbor in September 1779. Nature came to Nevis' rescue, when a hurricane slammed into the island and d'Estaing's fleet, sinking several of his ships, damaging the rest, and causing him to withdraw from the Caribbean. His lost ships have never been found.

French Admiral Count d'Estaing

Events remained reasonably calm until 1782. Early that year, a 28-gun British frigate, *HMS Solebay*, was being pursued by three French warships, and was desperately attempting to reach the protection of Nevis' shore batteries, when she ran aground on a reef off the southern coast of the island. The French ships began firing into her as she lay aground; and, rather than lose her, the captain ordered her burned, and escaped to shore in longboats with the entire crew. When the fire reached her powder magazine, she blew up.

Only a week later, a column of nearly 50 ships was sighted standing for the island, led by French Admiral Count François de Grasse, in the 130-gun ship of the line *Ville de Paris*, the most powerful warship on earth. De Grasse and his fleet made for Fort Charles, passing within range of her cannon, but going on to anchor in St. Kitts. De Grasse held his fire, and the gunners at Fort Charles wisely did the same, knowing that the fleet could easily destroy the fort if fighting broke out. De Grasse carried an invasion force of over 5,000 to St. Kitts in order to take Brimstone Hill, "The Gibraltar of the Caribbean". The British were losing the war in North America, and, if Brimstone Hill fell, all the British West India colonies might be lost to them as well.

The 130-gun ship "Ville de Paris"

A necessary part of this plan was keeping Nevis in French hands while Brimstone Hill was besieged. De Grasse sent a warship to Nevis, demanding its surrender. With only 300 militia available, and many worn cannon in her forts, Nevis had no choice but to surrender. De Grasse gave very generous terms. After being presented with "ten fat sheep" by the President of the Nevis Council, de Grasse stated that additional gifts of food would displease him, as he would be forced to refuse them. He could see that Nevis was so impoverished that it could not afford to give up any edibles. He wrote to the President: "I am much affected at the scarcity which your island finds itself in for the support of your negroes".

A small garrison of French troops, under the command of Lieutenant Millon de Villeroy, was placed in Fort Charles. The original number was to have been only six men, but at the request of President Herbert of the Nevis Council, the size was increased. Herbert wrote de Grasse that he feared the slaves would rise against a small French force, especially if English ships appeared. De Grasse agreed, and sent a warship to take all of Nevis' good cannon to use at Brimstone Hill against the English. After 35 days of fighting, Brimstone Hill fell. Very shortly afterwards, the Treaty of Versailles was signed, and Nevis returned to British rule.

20

In 1787, Captain Horatio Nelson of the Royal Navy, was dispatched to the West Indies. His first assignment was to enforce the British Navigation Acts in Nevis, which he did with customary vigor. He seized three American vessels flying the British flag, illegally, and impounded their cargoes. The cargoes belonged to Nevis merchants, who promptly sued Nelson. The suit was decided in Nelson's favor, and the man who assisted him, President Herbert of the Nevis Council, introduced Nelson to his young widowed niece, Frances Herbert Nisbett. Shortly afterward, the two were married at Montpelier Plantation, with the Duke of Clarence, later King William IV, acting as Nelson's best man. The night before the wedding, a band of hungry runaway slaves stole the ox being fattened for the wedding feast, and ate it themselves.

Admiral, Viscount Nelson, Duke of Bronte

The United States became a major trading partner with the West Indies after the Revolutionary War. Alexander Hamilton, born in Nevis in 1757, was instrumental in the American victory and became the first Secretary of the Treasury of the United States. As such, he kept an eye on American trade with his birthplace. The Department of the Navy was formed in 1795, and three medium-sized frigates were built. This navy had not only never won an engagement, it had never even fought a battle. In 1799, the United States and France became involved in a undeclared war. One of the three frigates, the 38-gun *USS Constellation*, was dispatched to the West Indies to protect American shipping from French commerce raiders.

On 9 February 1799, *Constellation* was patrolling north of Nevis, when another warship was sighted. She was the 40-gun French frigate *L'Insurgente*, the most daring and dangerous of the French raiders. She had already captured six American merchant vessels. *Constellation* challenged her and set off in pursuit, when she changed course and made for the neutral Dutch island of Saba. The chase lasted three hours, during which time the French ship was struck by a rain squall and lost her main topmast. This slowed *L'Insurgente* and hampered her agility. *Constellation* overtook her about a mile and a half off the southeast coast of Nevis. With all her guns bearing, she fired a broadside into *L'Insurgente*, which returned fire at once. Except for the damage to *L'Insurgente*, the vessels were evenly matched and battled furiously for an hour and a half, at which time *L'Insurgente* struck her colors and surrendered. Nevis was the site, not only of the first United States naval battle, but of its first victory as well.

The 19th Century in Nevis saw Emancipation, the end of military activity and failure of the sugar economy. Two more attacks were made upon Nevis by French forces: one in 1805, and another in 1806, led by Jerome Bonaparte. That was the last military offensive to be made against the island.

The militia was disbanded in 1838, and the forts were abandoned in 1854. Economic decline and growing American power put an end to European colonial adventures in the Caribbean.

In spite of increased demand for sugar, Europe and North America, by the 1820's, produced much of their own needs, and new sugar producing colonies in the British Empire drove prices steadily downward. Emancipation brought freedom to 8,815 slaves in Nevis, and compensation of 151,006 pounds to their masters. The slaves received nothing for their years of servitude, and faced a steadily deteriorating economic situation. The average wage for a laborer in Nevis was five pence per day, at a time when it cost four pence per day to feed a prisoner in an English jail. The result was a mass migration outward, and a subsequent decline in population.

The economy staggered on until the 1890's, when the situation suddenly worsened. The Nevis sugar industry picked up during World War I, but collapsed almost totally in the 1920's and 1930's, when estates were abandoned and the government confiscated them for non-payment of taxes. Some of the steam mills continued to crush cane in small amounts; the last ceased operation in 1958. In 1883, the Nevis government was abolished and amalgamated with St. Kitts. For the first time in 258 years, Nevis no longer had a local government. This situation remained until 1983, when the Nevis Assembly was reconstituted and local self-government returned.

By the 1930's, the Caribbean was considered an "Imperial Slum" – a far cry from the 1770's, when Willam Pitt declared that four–fifths of Britain's overseas wealth derived from the West Indies. Britain belatedly recognized its obligation to the region in the 1930's, when agitation for better living and working conditions began to surface, and West Indians began speaking out. The Moyne Commission was established, and sent to the Caribbean to assess the situation and make recommendations for improving living conditions. It visited Nevis on its tour. Many recommendations were delayed in implementation by World War II, but its most significant and long-lasting contribution was in the area of public health. The mosquito-borne diseases of yellow fever and malaria were eliminated, and health conditions and life expectancy improved dramatically.

During World War II, enough money was voluntarily collected in St.Kitts and Nevis to purchase two Spitfires for the RAF during the Battle of Britain. Nevis sent a number of men to serve in the British armed forces. Conditions were very hard in Nevis during the war years. Flour, especially, was in very short supply. In the years after the war, it was noted, that only five Europeans were resident in Nevis. An attempt was made during the 1950's to replace sugar with coconut and cotton production, but met with only limited success.

Even though money was always in short supply in the 19th Century, the Methodist and Anglican churches established church schools, and attendance was rigorously enforced. When government took over the education system, its excellence continued. In Nevis, approximately 22% of revenue is spent on schools; the largest single item in the island's budget. The success of

Cotton Gin

this approach is evident in the Federation's literacy rate of 98%, the highest in the western hemisphere.

In 1970, a tragedy occurred which affected almost every family in Nevis. Returning from Basseterre, the ferry M.V. *Christena* sank off Nag's Head. It was badly overloaded, and began taking water rapidly in the channel. Before any orderly evacuation could be accomplished, it started sinking by the stern, and, as it went down, capsized, trapping passengers inside. Many occupants were unable to reach life preservers, and 209 people drowned. Valiant efforts were made by boats in the area to pick up survivors, but the suddenness of the accident and the numbers of people involved, made substantial rescue impossible. A plaque in the Gingerland Methodist Church gives the names of 14 church members who perished in the accident, and illustrates how the tragedy touched the entire island.

In the 1960's, Britain created the Federation of St.Kitts, Nevis and Anguilla and granted it limited self-government. The seat of the Federation was in St.Kitts, and Robert L. Bradshaw was elected the first Prime Minister. Anguilla soon left the Federation and Nevis has the constitutional right, on a two-thirds public referendum, to leave the Federation and become independent should it choose to do so. On 19 September 1983, the Federation became independent of Great Britain and joined the Commonwealth.

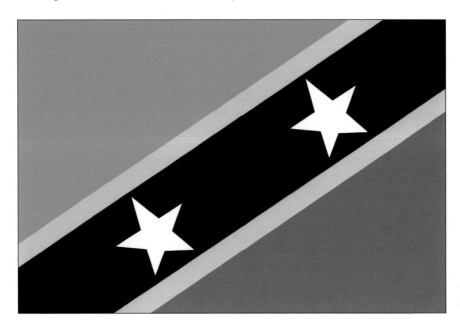

*National Flag of
St. Kitts and Nevis.*

Since the Federation was created and independence granted, prosperity is returning to Nevis after many long and painful years of relative poverty. This improvement has been due more to education than to any other single factor. Many Nevisians migrated to England, America and Canada, and to other Caribbean islands. Because of their high level of education, they prospered and sent money back to their families in Nevis. Remittance money literally kept the island afloat in the mid-20th Century.

Tourism has grown significantly in the last decade, but not to the point where it has overwhelmed local culture. Government has wisely required tourist facilities to be of top quality only, and has avoided the mass tourism which has spoiled so many other Caribbean Islands. Government is also encouraging the development of Nevis as a sophisticated offshore financial center, to create another source of income. Again, because of the high level of local education, these endeavors have met with success.

Looking at gentle Nevis today, it is difficult to imagine it as having once been the focal point of European imperial conflicts, the site of significant military engagements and immense wealth. Its past was often violent, tragic and brutal. Nevisians today can be proud that they have lifted the island out of the wreckage left after the collapse of the sugar economy, and are charting a course to future prosperity.

Uniform Corps Parade for the Seventeenth Anniversary of Independence

A VISITOR'S HANDBOOK

Only a few hours suffice to convince the visitor that in Nevis he has found a place of unique beauty and charm, a place which will grow on him with each new discovery. The original Carib inhabitants called it "Oualie", or Land of Beautiful Water. The native pronunciation of Nevis is "Nee-vis".

First, there is an intimacy with nature which awakens all the senses: the gentle warmth of the sun; the cool breath of the Tradewinds; the limpid turquoise sea, ever near; the endless horizon; the riotous colours of bougainvillea with its red and purple and orange bracts, the flaming Royal Poinciana; the sounds of birds and bees and chirping things; the pandemonium of farmyard animals at daybreak; the unsolaced solo of the mourning dove at nightfall; the juicy sweetness of a freshly-picked mango; the silky-smooth texture of a jelly coconut.

The beach at Hurricane Hill

Then, there is the welcome, Nevis-style, with smiles and quiet hospitality that make you feel you are an invited guest to this island: You, here, now. It is the people who make the difference. There has always been a kinship, however polite and proper, between Nevisians and visitors. The experience is one of coming home to traditional values, even a tinge old-fashioned, so often lost in the ruthless pursuit of financial success. Dress is informal, so there are few obvious distinctions between haves and have-nots. It is relaxing to be totally acceptable everywhere, as is, and to leave one's hang-ups behind.

Welcome to a country where there is virtually no crime, where police are not armed – except for certain coastal patrols – and are generally more helpful than coercive. However, parking tickets at $100 E.C. do exist, so mind the curb markings! This is a society determined to remain drug free, with harsh sanctions of up to $100,000 E.C. and 5 years imprisonment for those who dare to flirt with the law.

Welcome to a country with the highest literacy rate in the Western Hemisphere: Ninety-eight percent of Nevisians read and write proficiently. (Overhearing the local lingo spoken among friends on the street, you might have to strain to catch the gist of the conversation. Calypso English has a different lilt!) Poetry and the Classics are frequently recited, debating teams compete in regional contests, and writing ability is encouraged from earliest grammar school. The British school system affords students a rigorous program which prepares them for advanced studies, usually at the University of the West Indies, the University of the Virgin Islands, or in the United States, Canada or Britain. For those who enter the workworld, the level is roughly equivalent to completion of junior college.

Welcome to a health-conscious society where heart disease is rare, and smoking is almost non-existent, even in bars and restaurants. The chief medical officer at the hospital confirms that eating disorders and the "pathologies of affluence" are largely absent in the local population. Cleanliness is a habit of daily life, and great attention is given to a neat appearance: witness the impeccably dressed and groomed school children, even at play. Sunday is an occasion to "go all out" in sartorial finery. Pristine white, from head to toe, is *de rigueur* in certain churches.

In Nevis, the spontaneous is routine. How restrictive to adhere to a meticulous plan when one can "go with the flow", and allow the unexpected to happen. An elderly resident, once the town shoemaker, told me with no uncertain glee: "I surprised my mother at birth, as she was expecting a girl . . . and I have been surprising people ever since!" Disconcerting at first, this penchant for the "happening" becomes a source of anticipation and delight. This is not to say that serious matters do not receive timely attention: Bank and store hours, business appointments, transportation schedules and taxi drivers may be relied upon for exactitude.

What might be considered a humdrum occupation elsewhere, takes on a sense of worth and importance in this well-integrated and harmonious society. Each profession, each endeavor, is worthy of respect as a "job well done". Sloppiness and shoddiness are simply not tolerated, and squandering of precious resources is severely reprimanded. Old folks remember when a ha'penny was worth something!

Charlestown Post Office

Social interaction has its rules in Nevis. When a point is to be made, or a favor asked, one begins by inquiring about the other's health, family or business. Here, a word of caution to the wise: Almost all Nevisians are related in some way, and the person you are talking to is very likely to be the cousin of the person you are talking about. Besides, there is a sense of caring and responsibility towards one's physical neighbors, one's clients, a first loyalty which may mean that everyone cannot be accommodated at once. The corollary of this social cohesion is that rumors circulate at the speed of light, kindled by natural inquisitiveness and concern. A favourite forum for news and gossip is the Post Office at mail pick-up time.

Nevisians share a proud awareness of the remarkable features of their island as seen from the air, the sea, and the land, as well as a deep respect for the "genius of the place". Caring for the environment is very much an individual concern, contributing to a rising level of public consciousness about the preservation and development of natural resources. Close cooperation between non-profit organizations and the Nevis Island Administration has brought results in prohibiting illegal sandmining, cleaning up beaches and appointing litter wardens.

The Nevis Division of the St. Kitts & Nevis Chamber of Industry and Commerce has launched the "Charlestown Initiative", a far-reaching program to tap international resources such as the U.S. "Main Street Project" in matters of urban preservation and renewal, and to mobilize the business community to create a safe, practical and beautiful downtown area for locals and visitors alike.

The Nevis Historical and Conservation Society, founded in 1980, has led the effort to preserve the cultural life and historical heritage of the island. In 1988, with support from the World Wildlife Fund, the group began monitoring fragile and threatened areas that include coastal lands, wetlands, and uplands. NHCS also operates the Museum of Nevis History in the Alexander Hamilton house, and the Nelson Museum, acts as a "national trust" maintaining the archives and library of Nevis history, carries out research and archeological digs, and publishes a widely-read newsletter.

When it comes to Ecotourism, Nevis prones the philosophy that a healthy natural environment generates a sustainable tourism market. As you become better acquainted with Nevis and its people, and perhaps begin to identify with their values, it is hoped that you, too, will want to preserve and promote your discovery so that it remains a living treasure for generations to come.

TRADITIONS AND CUSTOMS

Two very special festivities rhythm the Nevisian calendar: Culturama, from the last Thursday in July to the first Monday in August, and Carnival Celebrations, from Christmas Eve to the day after New Year's.

CULTURAMA is a time of homecoming for expatriate Nevisians, wherever they may live for reasons of education, profession or family. Guests from abroad are also invited to share in this festive portrayal of traditional life in Nevis. Activities are so numerous and engaging that it takes considerable stamina to survive the entire fortnight! 'Round-the clock festivities culminate in a seafaring party on J'ouvert Morning when revelers "jam" until they drop.

Miss Culturama 2000

In 1974, members of the Nevis Drama and Cultural Society, along with other enlightened citizens, set out to preserve and revive traditional folklore, arts and crafts, and musical talent.

During the first decade, funds were raised to build a cultural center at Grove Park where theatrical productions and concerts are now held. In 2000, the defunct Paramount Cinema was renovated to accommodate indoor productions. Local artists display paintings, pottery, handmade linens, basketry and woodwork through Charlestown. The Cultural Village comes to life, and colourful booths serve up a movable feast of local specialities: barbecued chicken and ribs, conch fritters and chowder, goat water, rotis, patties, corn on the cob and homemade pies and cakes.

Every evening, crowds flock to the open-air theatre to attend the Youth Talent Show, the Beauty Pageant (including a much-ballyhooed bathing suit contest), and the Calypso Competition. Musical entries are aired on the radio for weeks, and excitement builds up to the final night when contestants rival one another with elaborate costumes and staging for the title of "Calypso Monarch". Strutting roosters, bridal parties in drag and other preposterous antics keep the audience rocking with laughter and applause. The winner is assured of the Number One spot on the VON (Voice of Nevis) Hit Parade and throughout the Leeward Islands.

CARNIVAL, or CHRISTMAS SPORTS, derives its inspiration from ancient African rituals brought to Nevis by plantation workers centuries ago. Prior to Emancipation, Christmas Sports provided an outlet for traditional narratives, dancing, music, food and religious practices which were suppressed by the prevailing European culture. The players evolved a rich oral tradition, and succeeded admirably in exposing – through myriad disguises and impersonations – the gross injustice, social hypocrisy and moral deficiencies of the upper-class plantocracy. Today, the Sports are not only an expression of this heritage, but a living repository which has grown to include such diverse influences as the American Western and Tarzan of the Apes. Despite their outwardly fanciful and outrageous form, these proverbs and rhymes serve as an effective linguistic tool in provoking serious thought about obvious truths and familiar experiences.

The remembered delight of Christmases past is evident in these recollections of a Nevisian friend: "You didn't have to see them to know they were coming! Troupes of masqueraders wearing trinkets and Christmas bells could be heard from afar, backed by the melodious sounds of a string or steel band and the driving beat of the big drum".

Traditional masquerade dancers

The parade in Charlestown

"Here and there, they would stop and have displays. Biblical stories, like David and Goliath, were classics. Slugging matches would break out, and the Sergeant would arrive to pacify and handcuff the belligerents. Clowns and Mummies and Bulls entertained the throngs crowding the streets."

"Most fantastic of all was the Sagwa Group, which picked up on real-life events during the year and mimicked them right in your own backyard: Neighborhood feuds, wayward husbands, pillow-stuffed pregnant daughters trying to fool their parents into believing they had done no wrong . . . anyone was fair game for public ridicule. They brought suitcases of costumes. And when the music stopped, they would change around and commence a new scene. There were amazing stunts and acrobatics, and the rhythm really went to your head. It was hilarious!"

"Other troupes included the Carib Indians, fierce and vicious savages dressed very scantily. They could not be controlled. Moving like they were crazed. Jumping on roofs. You never knew where they were coming from nor when they would rush the crowd, sending terrified children running to their Mommy. Shoes were left behind for speed and agility. No one to save you, either; just your luck. Policeman would stand back and laugh at your predicament. Cowboys would clatter into town on horseback, spinning pop guns and shooting from their holsters, while Indians in feathered headdress gave blood-curdling war whoops. They studied the Westerns at the local cinema and knew their moves to perfection."

"Traditional dance troupes, beautifully dressed in floral prints and shimmering velvet performed the Cake Walk and the French Quadrilles, just as they did in the old days for the pleasure of plantation owners and their guests." Today, house-to-house carol singing by church groups brings Christmas cheer to the elderly and homebound, and Carolfest brings together all the musical talent of Nevis in a night-long celebration of Christ's birth.

Moko-jumbies, who originated hundreds of years ago in Guinea, West Africa, are being revived today in carnivals throughout the Caribbean. Towering twelve feet into the air on wooden stilts, defying the laws of balance as they dance and sway, they are thought to escape the gravitational forces of the earth. The analogy suggests that by performing these amazing feats, man has the ability to escape the traps which life sets for him. Moko-jumbies, literally "doctors of the spirit", are thought to protect people from evil in the New Year, and are loved by young and old.

Yuletide fare features such festive foods as spit-roasted suckling pig, rice and peas, cassava bread, johnnycakes and blood pudding. Christmas red sorrel is the typical tipple of the Season. Served fermented or unfermented, it is a rather bland drink until properly doctored up with spices and a generous dose of rum. This is indeed a perfect time to join in the fun and merrymaking, to partake in customs as rich as fruitcake, to revel in festivities as colourful as Carnival, to feel the warmth of the Christmas spirit without having to bundle up. In sum, to enjoy Nevisian hospitality at its holiday best.

RELIGION

Religion, both in content and structure, has always played a central role in the life of Nevis. The island is divided into five parishes: St. Thomas' Lowland; St. James' Windward; St. Paul's Charlestown; St. George's Gingerland; and St. John's Figtree. These Anglican churches were all founded in the Seventeenth Century by the English settlers. They were originally built of wood, and later rebuilt in local stone. Sephardic Jews and Quakers were also present in Nevis in the 1600's. In the early 1700's, Roman Catholics were banned by law from the island, and not fully rehabilitated until 1882.

Cornerstones, plaques and graveyards chronicle the lives of governors, bishops, missionaries and early original Nevisian families, whose names are carried on today. St. Thomas', built in 1633, is the oldest Protestant church in the Caribbean. St. James' Windward, first constructed in 1679, contains a rare crucifix with a black Christ. St. John's Figtree displays the marriage certificate of Lord Nelson, Britain's most famous admiral, on the occasion of his marriage to a Nevisian beauty, Fanny Nisbet, in 1787.

It was about this time that Methodist missionaries arrived in Nevis to evangelize both blacks and whites, and organized the first Sunday and Day School for children of slaves.

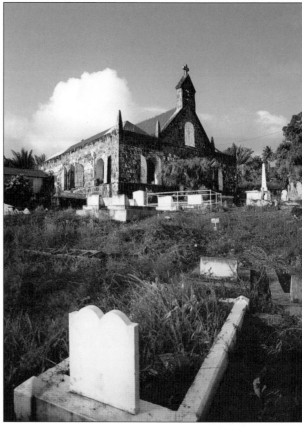

St. John's Figtree Anglican Church

The suspected connection to abolitionist movements led to the bombing, in 1797, of a Methodist chapel where the missionary, John Brownell, was preaching. In true Christian spirit, charges were not pressed, and no further acts of violence were reported. In 1826, church records show 802 members, 601 of whom were slaves.

Today, the Anglican Church remains dominant, although Methodists, Baptists, Seventh Day Adventists, Evangelical and Pentecostal sects have become very much a part of the religious scene. Whatever one's denomination, church-going is the norm in Nevis.

The religious content of Nevisian life can be felt in every area of human endeavor. Thanks and praise are often rendered to the "Almighty". Public meetings and conferences always begin with an invocation.on public occasions. The National Anthem contains the exhortation: "With God in all our struggles." And one frequently hears, "God willing", "God spare life", or "God bless you", as a parting remark. Special prayers are offered for the many Nevisians who sail upon the seas. Church communities welcome the visitor and inquire about his well-being on the island. The school day begins with an opening prayer in assembly, usually followed by a hymn. Ships are blessed and buildings dedicated.

All dressed up for Sunday School

Life in Nevis, for most people, is punctuated by these frequent hops to surrounding islands. Chances are, their mother, brother, aunt or cousin lives in St. Kitts, or maybe in St. Martin. Children go to spend the Summer with their grandma, and return laden with toys and gifts. Family reunions – a big thing throughout the Caribbean – bring long-lost relatives together. Besides the obvious social aspect, these family ties are often the basis for some sort of commerce.

The importance of the off-island economy cannot be overemphasized. The very nature and specificity of a small island engenders the need to trade. There is the access to a larger market: Fruits and vegetables growing in abundance in Nevis, furniture and other handcrafted objects, find their way to willing customers on other islands. Much-needed products can be made available locally. Besides the usual foods and supplies, clothing and domestic goods,

A Market Shop on Hanley's Road

there is a lively commerce in tools, auto parts, vehicles, appliances and building materials. This, in turn, sustains maritime shipping and its ancillary corps of stevedores, customs agents, dock workers and crew. The cargo trade, among man's most ancient economic activities, is not only thriving today, but is assured of tremendous development in the future. Another important aspect of the off-island economy is the funneling of funds back into Nevis from expatriates whose trade or professional competence has led them to settle elsewhere in the Caribbean, or in the United States and Canada, where large communities of Nevisians can be found.

Cattle enjoy green pastures

With the demise of the large sugar plantations, the economic pattern of land use has progressively changed. Agricultural activity on Nevis has become the domain of less than a thousand full-time farmers, who produce a range of crops such as yams, peanuts, carrots, cabbage, eggplants, cucumbers, tomatoes, peppers, pumpkins, peas and beans. They are aided by government programs which provide irrigation systems, tractors and harvesting equipment. What does not end up in Nevisian kitchens, is sent over to St. Kitts. Some sea island cotton is still grown and sold exclusively to Japan. Bamboo and climbing palms are being utilized in the production of bamboo and rattan furniture. The Nevis Beekeeper's Cooperative was organized in 1987, by a volunteer from the British Voluntary Service Overseas, and now numbers over 200 beehives.

From the large animal population used to work the sugar estates, livestock owners have turned to the production of domestic meats and by-products. There are currently only five large estates where grazing lands are available: two are government-owned and three are private. Poultry is raised throughout the island and is readily available in the markets. A modern abattoir, with complete cold storage facilities, processes the livestock for consumption. Many families keep small herds of goats and sheep for domestic use. Pigs and chickens are also raised in the backyard. Fishing activity is still very productive in the waters surrounding Nevis. Fishermen and lobstermen set traps, or "pots", three or four miles offshore, which they check on a regular basis, or employ nets, spears or trawling methods. The Nevis Fishing Cooperative provides cleaning and cold storage facilities.

The "Caribe Breeze" celebrates its first year of operation

A FISH STORY

One Saturday morning about 10:00 A.M., the author and photographer could be observed waiting expectantly on the beach at Indian Castle, scanning the horizon for the tiny dot of a fishing boat returning with its catch. Brooker and Teddy and the others had set out before dawn with the hope of bringing in a bumper crop of lobsters. It has something to do with the full moon and the tides and the sex life of crustaceans.

We were not disappointed! Shimmering and slithering fish in the morning sun, and lobsters cringing furtively under the prow, made for an awesome catch. The dazzling array of colours led me to fancy that the Creator had dipped into the rainbow's palette to paint these beautiful swimmers: Red and yellow-tailed snappers, hinds, wrenchmen, wahoos and the technicolor toms, in vivid and exotic hues. The variety of shapes and markings was astounding. We couldn't resist the temptation to pick them up and admire their features. "Watch out for the Old Wife's gaping jaw!" we were warned: "She is vicious . . . but delicious."

Everyone gave a hand to haul the heavy boat onto the beach. Repeated "Heave-ho's" were necessary. Many smiles and photos later, the happy crew packed the miraculous catch into waiting ice chests, and drove off to the market just in time for the throngs of Saturday shoppers.

Fish market at Charlestown, on Gallows Bay

The colourful catch.

HORSE RACING IN NEVIS

By Richard Lupinacci, President, Nevis Turf & Jockey Club

At least ten times each year, Nevisians assemble on the scenic southern coast at Indian Castle for an afternoon of local horse racing. For many years, the races were held on the five Bank Holidays (Boxing Day, Easter Monday, Whitmonday, Emancipation Day/Culturama and Independence Day); but in recent times, due to popular demand, the Nevis Turf & Jockey Club (formalized in 1967) has had to organize additional meets. A typical race card will have six races starting in mid-afternoon and ending at dusk. An average of four horses is in each race, which runs in the traditional British clockwise direction on a five-furlong oval, with a gentle but challenging hill up to the homestretch. Distances range from 5.5 to 8 furlongs. There is an old-fashioned flag start which offers moments of tension, frustration and comic relief.

Huge crowds turn out for an event which dates from the earliest days of the island's history. The appreciation of "blood horses" and horse racing stirs through most Nevisians as far back as anyone can remember. It is part folk festival, part Caribbean carnival with music, food, refreshments, and great high spirits. It is not uncommon to find three or four generations of a single family, from lively great-grandmothers to nursing infants. Everyone mixes, with no social barriers, and the mood is West Indian life at its most jovial.

But, make no mistake, the races are the main attraction; and no matter what flirtation or debate is going on, everyone rushes to the rail when the horses appear! No one wants to miss a moment of the action. Each Nevisian has a favourite horse or owner or trainer or jockey and feels a personal involvement in the race. Most owners have only one or two horses which they feed, groom, train -- and sometimes even jockey themselves. International observers have noted the exceptionally good condition of the mounts and the skillfulness of the local jockeys, as well as the remarkable enthusiasm of the crowd. In 2000, Nevis was invited to join the prestigious West Indies Thoroughbred Racing Association, formed by the multi-million dollar racing authorities in Trinidad, Jamaica and Barbados.

THE SPORT OF DOMINOES

How can a game which is played sitting around a table for hours and hours be considered a sport? Well, just ask any amateur about "sportsmanship", and he will immediately think of dominoes . . . such is the fascination, mental energy and prowess spent on this game.

Pass by the fire station or one of the local shops, especially on Fridays and Saturdays, and you will hear the slamming of dominoes and the heated commentary of onlookers until the wee hours of the morning.

The venue is never fancy. It could be a few soda crates and a piece of plywood. Sandy's serves up crispy fried chicken to the regulars at Brown Hill, and other shops have a good supply of cold drinks on hand. Few accoutrements are needed: the intensity of the game is the thing.

Partners hone their mind-reading ability in order to enhance a winning strategy. Signs and signals are banned in the realm of "sincere dominoes". The game lends itself to a wide range of skills: finesse, innuendo, quick reflexes, and a high degree of concentration. The competitiveness of West Indian dominoes brings tremendous satisfaction to all players of this deceptively-simple game.

Saturday night at the Station

Pam and B.B. welcome guests to Golden Rock Estate

The Indians who lived on the island when Christopher Columbus arrived did not survive the successive waves of colonization and quickly died out, either because they contracted diseases brought in from Europe, or because of ill-treatment on the part of the invaders.

Throughout its history, Nevis has been settled by peoples of many nationalities and religions: After the Indians came the Spaniards, the British, the French, the Dutch -- of Catholic, Protestant or Jewish descent -- as well as a variety of adventure-seekers, who had fled for political reasons, or came to bury a shady past and make a fortune from the sugar cane culture.

Because of the extensive development of agriculture in the Caribbean, especially sugar cane, the African slave trade flourished from 1500 to 1860. This multiracial society had a rigid hierarchy, from the large plantation owners who wielded political and economic might, to the slaves who lived in unbearable poverty.

At the zenith of sugar production in Nevis, 10,000 of the island's 23,000 acres were devoted to cane. To meet the strong demand for farm labor, many black slaves were brought to the island. They rapidly outnumbered the European plantation owners. Only through terror was the minority plantocracy able to keep the upper hand, ruthlessly crushing the slaves' attempts at rebellion. However, after centuries of suffering, their descendants can at last see justice being rendered.

Although land remained in the hands of the planter class following Emancipation in 1838, the collapse of the world market signaled the demise of the large estates. By the time the last sugar mill was shut down in 1958, much of the land had been divided into smaller parcels for homesites and for agricultural use by former sharecroppers. Today, 80% of the homeowners in Nevis hold title to their lot. Since Independence, Nevisians have developed sound policies in the management of their natural and cultural heritage, thus restoring their island to a modern-day semblance of paradise lost.

The present population figure stands at 10,500 inhabitants, not counting native Nevisians living abroad, which would increase this figure two-fold.

Thanks to better standards of living and hygiene, the infant mortality rate on the island has significantly decreased in the past decades. The population is very young, and there are many beautiful and healthy children to symbolize the happiness and rejuvenation of the Nevisian people.

Apart from the native population, there is a small community of expatriate Americans and Europeans, who live in Nevis on a temporary or permanent basis. Some stay and work for only a few years; others choose to settle there for the rest of their lives; and some are the descendants of the original colonizers. But the bond among all these people is a common love for this, their island.

Sunday at St. Paul's Anglican Church

Don and Carol Peterson have spent more than thirty years on the island. They have a passion for plants, and especially, Hibiscus. Their nursery, "Absolutely Bushed", manages projects from landscaping to interior decorating, including the Charlestown Waterfront Promenade.

Robert Humphreys takes his inspiration from the indigenous fauna of Nevis, and sculpts with imagination and exquisite detail. His "Pelican" graces the Walwyn Plaza in Charlestown.

Sixth-formers prepare for A levels in the Public Library.

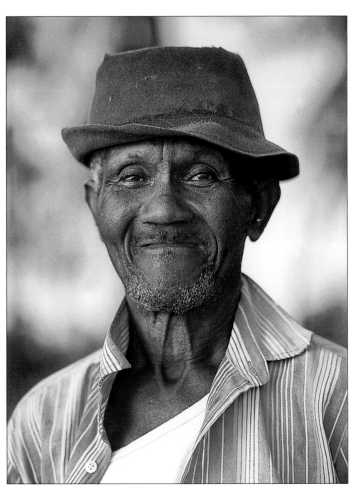

Mr. Martin was a fisherman,who became a Christian after a miraculous survival at sea. Every evening, he goes to the beach for a swim, and to admire the beauty of the sunset at Jessups Bay.

A Nevisian Beauty

This fisherman catches his dinner with a gossamer net at sundown on Pinney's beach.

Vincent Hubbard is the past-President of the Nevis Historical and Conservation Society, and an amateur archaeologist from the team which excavated the Jewish Synagogue in Charlestown, and many other sites.

This juicy fruit is the local chewing gum. Children always know where to find a guinep tree growing.

Woodcraft is an important activity on the island. A Nevisian cabinet maker, Paitfield Hill, displays a finely-sculpted bedpost.

Quentin Henderson was sent in 1987, by Voluntary Service Overseas, (the British Peace Corps), to develop beekeeping as a small industry on the island. The earliest reference to bees in Nevis dates from 1716. For many years, people known as "honey cutters" collected the honey from wild nests as a marginal activity. Today, the production of honey and beeswax candles is a fast-growing industry.

Nevis boasts two gold medal equestrians at the Special Olympics World Games in North Carolina. Here, Leon Silcott sports his Gold in Dressage, while Kishone Williams took first place in English Equitation and Showmanship.

When the Honey Bees String Band begins to play, you can't help but shake a leg!

These musicians craft their own instruments, according to age-old traditions, from local materials.

ARCHITECTURE

The climate and history of the Caribbean have developed an indigenous lifestyle, which, in turn, has an obvious influence on the architecture. For instance, most houses have a veranda and a natural ventilation system generated by air drafts. Louvered windows let the air in and out, cooling the house. The roof framework is raised high, to attract the air upwards. Basic construction materials were, and still are, volcanic stone and wood. Wooden buildings are lighter in structure and more fragile. Stone structures, being assembled with a coral powder cement, are sturdier and can better resist earthquakes. The usual building technique involves a combination of both materials. The ground floor is typically made of stone while the second story is wooden. This provides for greater comfort and security regardless of climatic conditions.

Coconut shingles

Volcanic stone

The Sand Box Tree in Charlestown

Bar shop in Caddock Road

One of Charlestown's characteristic features comes from the fact that, for centuries, maritime activity has been the basis of the economy. The main buildings all look out to the sea, and streets are parallel to the beach to make it easier for ships to unload freight. This typical pattern helps visitors understand what life was like in the past on this island, once among the most prosperous in the Caribbean.

The brightly-painted houses along the roads add a cheerful note to the landscape. They are raised off the ground on stone or brick blocks to let the water flow underneath. Another reason for this system is that houses must be transportable, as people do not necessarily own the land under their house.

Typical Nevisian House on Low Street

The Cotton Ginnery

The Henville Building

At some plantations such as New River Estate, Old Manor or Golden Rock, it is possible to visualize the sugar processing facilities in their heyday. Windmills are also part of the landscape. Their conic shape used to be a familiar sight all over the island. During the golden age of sugar production, it is said that there were up to 200 of them. Some were destroyed or are in ruins, but others have been restored and turned into elegant homes.

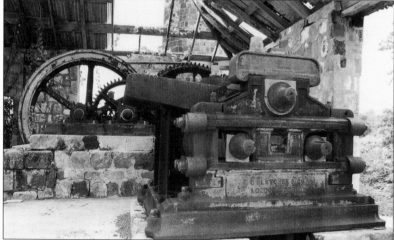

The sugar cane crusher at New River Estate

Silent Smokestack

St. Thomas' Lowland Anglican Church

A modern house in the spirit of the Caribbean to the north of the island

Churches are also typical of the island. There are several types of structures, some of wood, others of stone, or even cement. The oldest are the Anglican stone churches, built by the British settlers starting in the mid-17th Century. They have remarkably withstood the wear and tear of time. St. Thomas' church dates back to 1643. To this day, they are used as shelters during hurricanes.

The roofs of buildings are usually very wide because they are used to catch rainwater, which is filtered and stored in cisterns, before being boiled for domestic use. Regardless of the size of their house, Nevisians attach great importance to the exterior appearance, and especially to their gardens which usually abound with decorative flowers and plants. The rich volcanic soil of the island sustains a very luxuriant and diversified flora. Some amateur horticulturists have successfully started hibiscus, orchid and palm tree cultures.

Pool meets sea meets sky

CHARLESTOWN

By Daphne L. Degazon Hobson

Architect and Historic Preservationist

The chief town of the island, Charlestown, nestles along the eastern shore of an open bay or roadstead. With a present population of some 1,300 persons, it is the commercial, financial and administrative capital of the island and has both international and indigenous banks, modern telecommunications and car parking problems.

The narrow Main Street threads north-south through the historic towncenter on a meandering course. Small, two-story buildings of local stone and wood – many of which date from the early 19th Century – line the street and create the sturdy and picturesque character of the town. Modern concrete homes and business places are springing up on the outskirts and hills above the historic core.

At two places Main Street opens into a square. The larger one, "Courthouse Square" or "Memorial Square", is dominated by the stately Courthouse built circa 1815. The D.R. Walwyn Square was more recently named after a local son who, in the 1950's, opened the first indigenous bank, the Nevis Cooperative Bank located on Chapel Street.

The Bath Hotel

Government House

Many of the 18th Century stone houses collapsed during a series of disastrous earthquakes. This led to the practice of erecting an upper floor in wood over a stone ground floor. The tradition lasted into the 1950's, at which time the use of concrete blockwork was introduced for construction of the Charlestown Secondary School. Successive generations of Nevisians, however, succeeded in erecting and maintaining their most important and sacred buildings of two-storys in the abundant local stone: the Long Stone House (circa 1800), the Bath Hotel (circa 1804), the Courthouse (circa 1815), Government House (circa 1909) and the churches.

Court House and Library

The Methodist Church on Chapel Street is a monument to the capabilities and determination of the newly-freed slaves who funded and constructed it in 1844 – only 10 years after the abolition of slavery. The detailed tripartite entrance and dressed stonework is unique on the island. St. Paul's Anglican Church is a more modest structure built, rebuilt and restored over the years; its old cruciform plan and tombstones indicate an origin in the late 17th Century.

Few of the streets and alleys are sign-posted, but Nevisians know their town and expect to be asked for directions by visitors. Charlestown was built in slow-moving times, and the way to savour its qualities is to join in and stroll through its streets. You can't get lost!

St Paul's Anglican Church

Methodist Church

THE MUSEUM OF NEVIS HISTORY

The Georgian-style mansion housing the museum is built of volcanic stone and is the exact replica of the house where Hamilton was born in 1755. The house was reconstructed on the foundations of an old 1680 dwelling, which was probably destroyed during an earthquake in the 1840's.

On the ground level, there is a large exhibit hall displaying momentos of the island's history, from the Arawak Indians, to the sugar plantations, and up to the present time. There are also many artifacts and objects relating to the life of Alexander Hamilton. The second floor is used by the House of Assembly, the Nevis legislature.

Alexander Hamilton was born on January 11, 1755, the son of a Scotsman, James Hamilton, and a Creole, Rachel Fawcett. Alexander left Nevis at the age of eight and returned to St. Kitts in 1766. He was a bright student and had a real talent for numbers. At fifteen, he sailed off to America to go to

The Museum of Nevis History

school in Elizabethtown, New Jersey; he then went on to King's College, now Columbia University, in New York City. He was a patriot during the American Revolution, and became the first Secretary of Treasury under President George Washington. He was one of three authors of *The Federalist* papers, and was instrumental in shaping the political institutions of the United States of America: Executive, legislative and judicial. His most enduring monument is the preservation of the Union of the States as "one Nation under God, indivisible, with liberty and justice for all." His life ended tragically when he was shot on July 11, 1804, in a famous duel at Weehawken, New Jersey, with Vice-President Aaron Burr – of whom he had voiced a "despicable opinion" – and died the next day. He left a wife and seven children, heavily in debt. He was not yet fifty years old.

THE NELSON MUSEUM

The Nelson Museum is housed in a white stucco building located between the Bath Hotel and Government House. It features a well-documented collection of artifacts on Horatio Nelson. Reproductions of paintings, engravings and drawings, old costumes and a variety of objects recounting the brave deeds and love life of this extraordinary man are also displayed.

Horatio Nelson was born in England on September 29, 1758, to Reverend Edmund Nelson and Catherine Suckling Nelson. His mother died when he was only nine. He joined the Royal Navy at twelve as a midshipman aboard the *Raisonnable* commanded by his uncle, Captain Maurice Suckling. At the age of twenty, young Lt. Nelson himself became Captain and took command of the frigate *Hitchinbroke* in 1779.

It was not until 1784, however, that Nelson made his mark in the Caribbean as a staunch enforcer of England's Navigation Acts. Assigned to English Harbour in Antigua for the next three years, Nelson established himself as a force to be reckoned with when it came to illegal trading between the English colonies in the Caribbean and traders from the United States. An early assignment, in command of H.M.S. *Boreas*, brought him to Nevis. The culmination of Nelson's career in the region occured in 1785, when, passing near Nevis, he spotted four American ships trading just off Charlestown in violation of the Navigation Acts. He seized the vessels and impounded their cargoes. The Nevis merchants who owned the freight sued Nelson, but the Court decided in Nelson's favor.

It was at Nevis' Montpelier Estate in the late spring of 1785, that he met a young widow by the name of France "Fanny" Nisbet, and her son, Josiah. They fell in love and wed on March 11, 1787, at Montpelier, with the future King of England, Prince William Henry (William IV), giving away the bride.

Captain Nelson was assigned to the *Agamemnon* in 1793, and soon moved into the period of his life that established him as England's greatest naval hero. He had such skill at naval tactics that he has been called a genius by some. The "Nelson touch" refers to the many instances in which he was successful in battle. On October 21, 1805, off the coast of Spain near Cape Trafalgar, Admiral Horatio Nelson fought his most valiant battle. It was on this occasion that his famous phrase, "England expects that every man will do his duty", became a rallying cry for many generations to come. It was also the battle during which Nelson was shot, and died at the age of forty-seven.

200th Anniversary of the marriage of Nelson to Frances Nisbet

Montravers Estate

Nevis is an island for connoisseurs. People come here to relax and wind down. There are no traffic lights, no jams.Only a few hours suffice to circumnavigate the 20-mile main road, even allowing for photographs and a picnic.

The road winds and twists through the uplands on the leeward side, past the parishes of St. John's Figtree and St. George's Gingerland, then down to the lonely Atlantic shore, past Brick Kiln, St. James' Windward and Long Haul Bay.

Fields of sea cotton, dense coconut palm groves, forlorn ruins of sugar plantations, their machinery forever stilled, and the eerie shell of Eden Brown Estate, scene of an 18th-century duel, provide a running narrative. Tiny hamlets, bearing names like Chicken Stone or Hard Times, tell their own story.

Friendly minibuses ply the roads of Nevis, never failing to stop for a weary traveller, no matter how many passengers are already squeezed into the seats. They proudly announce their names in bold letters: "BADDA DAN DEM", "ONLY BELIEVE", "ROOTS", "EXODUS", "ZION TRAIN", or "SUPER CHIC".

From Charlestown going north, the first stop is at St Thomas' Anglican Church atop a prominent hill.

Tombstones at St Thomas' Anglican Church

Originally built in 1643, it is the oldest church in Nevis -- and may be the oldest surviving church in the English-speaking Caribbean. It contains a number of memorials to early settlers.

In the churchyard, the graves of planter families are oriented eastwards facing the rising sun. They overlook one of the most beautiful views of the sea. Further down the hillside, stands a school building whose roof was carried away by Hurricane Hugo in 1989, but which the Nevisians, ever anxious to preserve their heritage, are patiently restoring.

The view from Fort Ashby

Cottle Church

Continuing down the main road, one passes Nelson Spring on the right. The great number of artifacts found in the area suggests that this spring was already known to the Amerindians. However, its name comes from the fact that Captain Horatio Nelson supplied fresh water to his troops here in the 1780's. Opposite the spring is a beautiful mangrove surrounded by a coconut plantation.

A little further on the left, at Cades Bay, is Fort Ashby. It is one of the oldest forts on the island. Several cannons remain. Above the fort, climbing up towards the Nevis Peak, is one of several sulphur quarries. Steam sometimes escapes from fumaroles. It is a modern quarry which came into operation in 1951.

Figurines from the Newcastle Pottery

The black crucifix at St. James' Anglican Church

Continuing along the main road towards the airport, right after a long stretch of straight road, there is a yellow sign pointing to the right. About 500 yards, up a rocky road, one arrives at the charming Cottle Church. It was built in 1824, by John Cottle, the owner of Round Hill Estate which, at the time, covered an area of 980 acres. Cottle was President of Nevis and known as a gentle slavemaster. He built the church as a place of worship for his family and slaves, as the latter were not allowed to belong to any of the Anglican churches at the time. Unfortunately, erosion has by now badly damaged the structure.

In Newcastle, beyond the police station, stands a long grey concrete building. It is the Newcastle Pottery Factory, where all kinds of useful and decorative wares are made by hand, according to traditional methods. The clay comes from the nearby Potworks Estate, and the unique red color is obtained by adding crushed rock. The objects are fired over a bonfire fueled by coconut shells.

A few kilometers farther down the main road is St James' Anglican Church. Built in the late 17th Century, its earliest tombstone dates back to 1679. It is one of three churches in the Caribbean known to contain a black crucifix. The sanctuary floor contains many stone crypts where early Nevis settlers lay buried.

Eden Brown Estate is located just a few kilometers further south, after Butlers. Built around 1740, this estate is said to be haunted, after an incident in 1822. A duel took place between a Maynard (the groom) and a Huggins (the best man) on the day of Maynard's wedding to one Julia Huggins. Both men were mortally wounded, and it is said that Julia became a recluse. The estate was abandoned and eventually went to ruin.

Eden Brown Estate

New River Plantation

New River Estate lies southward on the left. Built as a sugar producing and processing plantation in the 17th Century, its machinery was converted to steam in the late 19th Century and continued operating until the 1940's. The standing ruins of the main buildings are still in excellent condition, especially the windmill machinery and the cistern.

Coconut Walk Estate is located along a side road leading down to the sea. It is probably the one sugar estate in the best state of preservation remaining on the island today. Some of the stone work dates back to the mid-18th Century. However, most of what is left standing was built between 1810 and 1834. It has the largest sugar mill on Nevis due to its position at sea-level, ideal for collecting wind. The coastline is rugged here, and offers visitors a chance to see the contrast between the windward coast and the leeward coast, with its calmer waters and sandy beaches.

Further up towards Nevis Peak, on the right, is Golden Rock Estate, now an inn. Most buildings have been carefully restored, and visitors may ask Manager Pam Barry to give them a guided tour of the old mill which has been transformed into a honeymoon suite.

Stonyhill Reservoir is close to the hotel. It is the starting point of a beautiful walk towards the main source of fresh water in Nevis. On the way up, one discovers the rainforest and its lush vegetation,

The Botanical Garden

colourful birds and butterflies; and, with a bit of luck, one may even encounter a playful group of Vervet monkeys. It is advisable to hire a guide for this tour, to be sure to see everything and to avoid getting lost.

Sunrise at Coconut Walk Estate

Back on the main road, at the Market Shop crossroads, turn left onto the secondary road leading down to Indian Castle Estate, now a government farm, where cattle and several experimental crops are raised. It was at one time a busy port, bustling with ships coming to load sugar and by-products for export to England, Canada and the United States. The racetrack is also located there along one of the wildest beaches of the island.

St George's Anglican Church

Fish traps at Indian Castle Beach

On the way back from Indian Castle, on the right, is St. George's Anglican Church, built circa 1842, with additions including a major reconstruction in the 1950's after an earthquake. The basic layout is typical of Anglican church architecture, with two large entrances and a central worship chamber. The earliest tombstone dates back to 1724.

The Gingerland Methodist Church, dating from 1801, stands after the crossing on the left. The present building, unusual for Nevis, was reconstructed in 1930. It is a Richardsonian-style octagonal shape, with intricate roof joists.

Saddle Hill is located to the south of the island. Getting there is difficult, however, and it is better to have a guide. A fortress, still in excellent condition today, was built in 1740, on a high promontory. Horatio Nelson is reported to have used this vantage point as a lookout for enemy ships.

Further down the road is a sign for the Hermitage Plantation Inn. Built around 1740, it is said to be the oldest wooden house still in use in the Caribbean. It has been meticulously restored by its owners, the Lupinacci family. An old cistern, water cooler and purifier, storehouse and stone walls can still be seen.

Opposite the Hermitage, follow the road to the Montpelier Plantation Inn. This magnificent building of volcanic stone seems to have remained untouched by time. This is where Horatio Nelson's wedding with Frances Nisbet took place on March 11, 1787. Farther on, follow signs to the Botanical Garden, with its Tea House and well-stocked Gift Shop.

Back on the main road, to the right, is St John's Figtree Anglican Church dating from 1680. The present building, however, was reconstructed in 1838, with additional work done in 1895. The marriage certificate of Horatio Nelson and Frances Nisbet is prominently displayed here.

BEACHES

The island is surrounded by magnificent beaches, each endowed with its own character and special charm. The most beautiful is certainly Pinney's Beach. The grey volcanic sand is very fine, and the coconut trees bordering the sea give an illusion of paradise. One is never disturbed by other bathers, as the beach is "endless". In fact, this is one of the Nevisians' favorite spots for family fun on Sundays and holidays. The Four Seasons Hotel is located at the very heart of this idyllic place. The bar offers visitors a wide range of delicious refreshments in a very elegant beach pavillion. Snorkeling gear and equipment for other nautical sports such as windsurfing, catamaran sailing, pedal boats, waterskiing, can also be rented there.

Herbert's Beach on the Atlantic Ocean

Opposite Nelson's Spring, beyond the Coconut Plantation, lies another lovely beach. Multicolored fishing boats rest on the sand, close to a hut of woven palm fronds that Robinson Crusoe would have loved.

Going north from Fort Ashby is yet another beautiful beach with a view of St. Kitts.

Oualie Beach is also very pleasant and an excellent spot for snorkeling. However, because of the strong currents flowing between St. Kitts and Nevis, it is best not to go out too far. The road linking Hurricane Hill to the airport winds along another tranquil beach.

Newcastle Beach (Airport in the distance)

Sailing into the sunset

On clear days, the view from the top of Nevis Peak is really breathtaking. It is the pinnacle of the island, and the 360 degree-view is unique. In order to ensure absolute safety, it is best to have a guide. Remember, there is no way of rescuing lost hikers, due to the steep slope and dense vegetation. Wear casual clothes and bring drinking water and cereal bars for a quick pick-up.

Mountain biking is a newcomer to Nevis

For those who like to spend time on the water, there are yacht charters: bare-boat, or with a seasoned skipper. There are also half-day sails to St. Kitts, with lunch and snorkeling included. Another possibility is to go deep-sea fishing with professional fishermen and try your luck with the Kingfish, Dolphin, Swordfish or Wahoo which abound in the deep waters around the island.

The undersea world is magical in its diversity, and offers dazzling landscapes. With snorkeling gear alone, bathers can see colourful fish and shellfish, including rock lobsters, and even a large conch or turtle on the sandy sea bed. Nevis is also an outstanding location for scuba diving, but it is advisable not to go out alone. For additional information, call SCUBA SAFARIS which specializes in scuba diving, delivers licences and organizes outings at sea. Some sites are caves, carved by corals, in which divers may see an ancient shipwreck or an abandoned anchor.

Snorkeling along the rocky coast

SHOPPING

All around the island, one finds a multitude of attractive little shops offering an assortment of sundries and daily provisions: canned goods, household products, cosmetics, cold drinks and snacks. Conveniently located along the main road, they are often indiscernible from neighboring Nevisian houses with their brightly-painted wooden exteriors and corrugated metal roofs.

In Charlestown, one finds a larger selection of grocery stores, including several supermarkets which carry a wide variety of items from frozen foods to floor-mops to Dom Perignon champagne!

In the covered market, local farmers display their fruits and vegetables, as well as homebrewed beverages and freshly-picked coconuts to "drink". Seasonal items make their debut here.

Along Main Street, and tucked away in courtyards, are boutiques which feature fashions appropriate for the island climate, such as T-shirts, sundresses, skirts, sandals and straw hats.

Fresh papayas

The Cotton Ginnery mall and restaurant

A showcase for local artists

Caribelle batik, hand-printed in gorgeous colors at the Romney Manor in St. Kitts, is available by the yard or made into flouncy skirts with matching blouses at Island Hopper.

Another locally-produced label, Island to Island, is the work of Canadian top designer, John Warden. The collection perfectly mirrors the gaiety and breeziness of the Caribbean in a variety of beautifully-made dresses, skirts, ensembles and beachwear.

On Saturdays, merchants sell ready-to-wear clothing from open vans, flea-market style.

Arts and crafts of high quality are produced in Nevis; Newcastle Pottery makes fired ceramic objects from simple vases to crockery pots to naïf animals and figurines.

Local artisans have a knack for making amusing and useful objects from all sorts of natural materials, such as coconut husks and seashells. Nevis Handicraft Co-op, close by the Tourism office, offers a large display of crafts and souvenirs at reasonable prices: feed-bag garments; woven-straw purses and totes; wall hangings; wooden bowls and utensils; and delicious homemade preserves, jellies, chutneys and the ubiquitous hot sauce.

Fragrant honey from tropical island flowers is produced by Nevisian bees and their keepers and sold in local shops.

A visit to the Philatelic Bureau is a must for serious stamp collectors and amateurs alike.

Local motifs guide the potter's hand

Sealife mobiles at the Nevis Craft House

Custom designed T-shirts

65

NEVIS-STYLE CUISINE

Whether for a traditional West Indian family meal or local fare at the inns and hotels of the island, good cooking begins with a choice of Nevisian produce from the open-air markets of Charlestown. Homegrown vegetables abound: breadfruit and christophine, eggplant and okra, pumpkin and yams, plantains and pigeon peas, tannia roots, avocados, and peppers both sweet and hot. Homemade pepper sauces rival one another for flavor and heat. Being a vegetarian here would be no hardship, as these delectables are turned into savory casseroles, soups and stews, fritters, purees, salads, relishes or the hearty rice dishes which round out each meal.

Almost every household has a few chickens, a resident pig who conveniently

Friday night barbecue at the Water Department

consumes the table scraps, and a family of goats or sheep. Island goats and sheep are often indistinguishable to a newcomer, but those in-the-know know: Goats' tails point up; sheep's tails point down. All these farmyard animals roam the countryside unfettered, eventually finding their way to the local butcher, and then to the cooking pot. Fragant curries, goat water, Saturday-night souse (pigs knuckles and trotters), smoky ribs, and versatile chicken – marinated, grilled, stewed or deliciously deep-fried in a crispy coating – are readily available. Reputations are made on "the best of" each specialty. Just ask a local!

Culturama, in late July, includes a week-long food fest on the waterfront to showcase culinary talent and sustain the calypso musicians and dancers through the night. The aromas are tantalizing on the evening breeze. Colorful stands feature meat or fish filled rotis, johnnycakes, spareribs, chicken or lambi (conch) to be downed with prodigious quantities of rum punch, Ting, or ice-cold Carib beer. Home brews include tangy ginger beer, sarsaparilla and maubi, prepared from tree bark.

Mutton on the hoof

Ribs-To-Go

The water around Nevis still yields an abundance of fish: kingfish, hind, flying fish, dolphin and snapper. The ubiquitous saltfish (salted cod) arrives in solid slabs from New England and points north. Saltfish finds its way into fritters, roti and rice dishes.

Most often, fresh fish are marinated in spices and lime juice before being broiled, steamed or stewed in a savory broth. Cooked until the bones "melt", stew fish are accompanied by fungi (cornmeal and okra dumplings) and homemade breads for dunking. Pepper sauce is a must at the table. You may see a Nevisian pop down a fish head with good-to-the-last-bite gusto.

Succulent Caribbean lobster is almost an everyday indulgence in local restaurants, appearing in salads and sandwiches, or classically grilled with parsley butter. More exotic versions include lobster baked in coconut milk, steamed with vanilla, or curried in stew. Fresh from the Caribbean Sea, this is a flavor and texture treat not to be missed by those of us accustomed to the frozen stuff.

Lobster fisherman

Glance upward into the trees for a visual foretaste of the dessert menu: mangoes, papayas, coconuts, sugar apples, oranges, grapefruit and bananas, ready to be consumed, as is, or to be transformed into fruit ices and creams, mousses and custards, cakes and pies. A favorite with the kids are guineps. They always know where to find guinep trees growing, and spend hours in the branches sucking the translucent pink pulp off the pit. The green clusters can also be purchased from roadside vendors. Can one really overdose on this fruitful bounty? When sunsweet treats are there for the picking, anytime seems appropriate to enjoy these healthy snacks. And what could be sweeter than a freshly-cut stalk of sugar cane from a nearby field, juice running down one's chin? For the more sophisticated amateur, imbibe the native Cane Spirit Rothschild in a fruity concoction.

Pick-up trucks will appear wherever there is a crowd, dispensing custardy fresh coconuts, opened with a flourish by a deft machete, providing both drink and food. Veritable "staff of life" for centuries in the Caribbean, the coconut palm was used for roofs, houses, rafts, ropes, cooking oil and soap, before making its way to the table. Puddings, pies and cakes, cookies and candies are just the beginning, as any piña colada fan will attest. Sweet or savory, the coconut finds its way into Nevisian kitchens in myriad disguises.

Whether shopping in the market or enjoying a meal anywhere on the island, it is easy to strike up a pleasant conversation with a farmer, fisherman, housewife or chef. You will tap a proud heritage of discerning quality, family secrets, and plantation recipes passed down through generations. You may hear tales of the sugar mill estates from retired overseers, or hurricane lore from lobstermen. Learn how to pick the perfect papaya, or open a coconut neatly. Sample "bush tea" and rare herbs: culinary, medicinal or aphrodesiac. You may be fortunate enough to glimpse behind the scenes the good-humored bantering which pervades the bustling kitchen. Take time to savour the smells, the taste, the colours of Nevisian cuisine, and it will whet your appetite for a lifetime.

Fresh coconut to eat and drink

RESTAURANTS

The restaurants of Nevis cater to a wide range of tastes, depending on your appetite, your mood and your sense of adventure. From the ultimate in luxury dining, or a romantic tête-à-tête in the hotels and plantation inns, to a family-style meal served up in friendly surroundings, to a barefoot beach barbecue of fish, lobster and burgers – all are available for the inquisitive visitor.

Unella's has the best view and seafood in Charlestown

A local eatery and night spot in Cotton Ground

This gastronomic sampler is "Grown in Nevis"

"Sunshine's" on the beach

OLD MANOR HOTEL

P.O. Box 70, Charlestown, Nevis, West Indies. Tel: (869) 469-3445 / Fax: (869) 469-3388. Reservations: 1-800-892-7093

The original machinery of the Estate

Old Manor Estate Hotel is located high on the slopes of Mt. Nevis in the Parish of St. George, in an area so lovingly called Gingerland. A ten-acre retreat of tropical gardens with fifteen guest rooms and a restaurant, all built within the restored stone ruins of the old sugar estate buildings. The old plantation's main water cistern has been restored to a unique round fresh-water pool, and the carriage house deck has been transformed into a tropical Jacuzzi for the comfort and enjoyment of guests. There is a small gift shop on the premises.

"The Cooperage" restaurant features fine dining in the casual atmosphere of the restored molasses warehouse and barrel-makers workshop, featuring an extensive variety of menu selections to suit all tastes.

Whether you hike to the rain forests or explore the many bridle paths and old plantation roads from the back of a horse, the scene is set to go back in time for a romantic, uncomplicated experience of life in the Caribbean at a slower place.

A spacious room in the main building

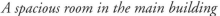

GOLDEN ROCK PLANTATION INN

P.O. Box 493, Charlestown, Nevis, West Indies. Tel: (869) 469-3346 / Fax: (869) 469-2113. Reservations: 1-800-223-9815

Eva Wilkin painting

The bridal suite inside the restored mill

Follow the narrow drive that winds through a grove of mango, breadfruit and banana trees, past the hollow draped with vines where vervet monkeys play, and enter a world of breathtaking beauty and gracious hospitality.

The feeling here is "cared for", be it the original sugar mill cum bridal suite, built in 1801, by Manager Pam Barry's ancestor, the seven secluded cottages filled with antiques and Nevisian artwork, the greathouse with its bounteous *table d'hôte* of local specialties, the shaded terrace with its view to faraway isles, the spring-fed pool that mirrors the turquoise sea, or the tennis court. Of particular note are the many original paintings by portraitist, Eva Wilkin, which grace the stone walls of the dining area and library. Additional works of this famous artist and lifelong resident can be seen at nearby Clay Ghaut Gallery. Most cared-for of all are the guests themselves. Virtually any request will be met by the helpful and informative staff.

In keeping with the island, activities are convivial and low-key. Guests are invited to participate in eco-rambles to the ruins of Coconut Walk Estate to learn about the history, archeology and ecology of Nevis, musical evenings with a string band, the "Honey Bees", craft days with local artisans, or self-guided hikes through the cloud forest to The Source. Afternoon tea and homemade cakes, or a soothing rum punch, always await the traveler. Golden Rock maintains its own outdoor restaurant at Pinney's Beach.

THE HERMITAGE PLANTATION INN

Gingerland, Nevis, West Indies. Tel: (869) 469-3477 / Fax: (869) 469-2481. Reservations: 1-800-682-4025

The Main House at Hermitage was built sometime between 1680 and 1740. Nevis Island lore calls it the oldest house on the island, and Jack Bertholet, author of the 1984 book, *Caribbean Style,* declares it the oldest surviving wooden house in the Caribbean. In twenty years of studying Caribbean architecture from Surinam to Cuba he had never found an older wooden house.

It was built as a small farmhouse before the days of large sugar plantations. The original owners were the Pembertons, from Pembroke in Wales, who likely experimented with various crops such as indigo, tobacco, cotton, spices and, eventually, sugar.

It was a small plantation of less than 100 acres situated 800 feet above sea-level. The land is stoney and strewn with boulders, with good soil in between. It was terraced into beds for cultivation, the extensive dry-stone walling remains one of the features of the plantation. There is no evidence of a sugar mill or factory, but there was a small animal-powered mill for grinding cane with horses, mules or oxen.

The strength and longevity of the house are due to the uncommonly strong mortice and tenon construction (heavily pegged at all joints), steep roof pitch design and extraordinarily durable lignum vitae timber framing. These heavy beams may have come from original Nevis trees, now extinct.

The property would have originally included the Main House, stone kitchen and ovens, water cooler and cisterns and other dependencies. The Main House is essentially as it was in the days when Nelson and Hamilton resided on the island.

In later years, the family prospered to own other estates all the way to the sea, and the original house was kept as a hillside residence for invalid members of the family. It passed from the Pembertons to the Maynards of Nevis in 1948, and in 1971, to the present owners.

Today, the Hermitage is a plantation inn and continues to offer traditional island hospitality and lifestyle for up to twenty-eight guests. The property reflects the owners' interests in island life with its original cuisine, reconstructed cottage rooms, collection of antiques, old-fashioned gardens, horses, carriages and local crafts and arts. It has become a "must see" for every visitor to the island. As a unique owner-operated hotel, it has recently been selected to be a member of the prestigious Romantik Hotels group. A charming boutique, "Fanny's closet", offers fashions by John Warden of St. Kitts, and a selection of local crafts.

MONTPELIER PLANTATION INN

P.O. Box 474, Charlestown, Nevis, West Indies. Tel: (869) 469-3462 / Fax: (869) 469-2932

The Main House

In the Seventeenth and Eighteenth Centuries, the plantations on the lush volcanic island of Nevis grew sugar cane. One such was Montpelier, named after Montpellier, France, by an exiled Huguenot who, after the revocation of the Edict of Nantes in 1685, had found life in his hometown untenable. Today the Plantation grows no cane and the buildings have been converted into a top class resort inn, small and exclusive. The French connection is not now so strong; Montpelier is owner-managed by an English couple, James and Celia Gaskell; but French is spoken, the wines are from France and various French influences are at work in the kitchen.

The aim of the owners is to give a good value holiday of high standard. They feel that what the guest wants is to be made welcome, to be treated as a special person, to feel safe and comfortable, to experience a sense of calm and tranquility, to eat and drink well, to meet other interesting and amusing people, to find beauty outside and good taste within, and to have enough to do and be able to enjoy a range of Caribbean sun-and-sea pursuits. The result is that you find here a rare combination of luxury and simplicity, a place whose beauty acts as a tonic to the stressed, a most friendly and delightful ambiance, all in an English country house party atmosphere – a home rather than a hotel.

You may spend the day at the Inn's exquisite private beach on the Caribbean side of the island, returning to the cool and lovely gardens of the Inn for tennis and afternoon tea. This is the Inn chosen in 1993, by the Princess of Wales for a family holiday with her two boys. It is a member of Romantik Hotels and Restaurants, the German-based group of small owner-managed properties of the highest standards.

NISBET PLANTATION BEACH CLUB

Newcastle, Nevis, West Indies. Tel: (869) 469-9325 / Fax: (869) 469-9864. Reservations: 1-800-742-6008

This historic plantation, built in 1778, is a rare blend of old-world elegance and modern tropical comfort.

In the Great House, guests may relax in the lounge or chat over a cup of tea. The main dining room on the veranda serves delicious meals in a very romantic atmosphere.

Bungalows are set on the green lawn in the midst of a coconut grove. Appointed with modern utilities and private screened balconies, they are extremely comfortable.

Down the tree-lined alley towards the beach lies a beautifully designed pool. Lunch is served in the informal "Coconuts" restaurant overlooking the pool. The beach, sheltered by a coral reef, is one of the most pleasant on the island, as waves break on the rocky barrier out at sea. The sea bed is covered with aquatic plants, and a great number of fish can be seen swimming in the crystal-clear waters. This is an ideal place for those who need to break away from their busy and stressful lives.

The coral sand beach

The bungalows and the Great House

The pool restaurant

Hibiscus

HURRICANE COVE BUNGALOWS

Oualie Beach, Nevis, West Indies. Tel: (869) 469-9462 / Fax: (869) 469-9462. Reservations: (306) 647-0333

This attractive complex seems to be clinging to the side of a small hill overlooking the sea, and offers an exceptional view of St. Kitts.

The self-catering bungalows are made of beautifully hand-finished wood with tile roofs and floors, tastefully decorated, and include a fully-equipped kitchen and covered porch. One gets a good feeling of the Caribbean spirit in the rooms, be they equipped with queen-size or twin beds.

The pool, built in the foundations of a 250 year old fortification, seems to be floating between sky and sea. The beach is only 3 minutes away, by foot, and is equipped with facilities for nautical sports.

The French windows and their shutters, the mosquito nets and the plants hanging from the ceiling provide for such harmony that one feels as if the hotel has always been there.

MOUNT NEVIS HOTEL AND BEACH CLUB

P.O. Box 494, Charlestown, Nevis, West Indies. Tel: (869) 469-9373 / Fax: (869) 469-9375. Reservations: 1-800-75-NEVIS

The hotel overlooks the small fishing village of Newcastle and is close to the ruins of Cottle Church. Built high on a hill, it offers a splendid view of the sea and nearby St. Kitts, in an absolutely peaceful and quiet setting.

Its tranquillity and modern facilities make it an ideal place to relax. All thirty-two rooms are equipped with air-conditioning, touch-tone telephones, cable TV and VCR. Each apartment has a kitchen and a private balcony where guests can have breakfast while enjoying the breathtaking view.

The main building includes a fine restaurant serving Continental and Caribbean cuisine. Down below is a large and beautifully-kept swimming pool, which allows sunbathing all day long.

A recent addition is the ultra-modern Conference Centre for groups up to 80 persons. It is fully equipped with air-conditioning, computers, and audio-visual aids, including power point and overhead projectors.

Down towards the sea, a few minutes from the hotel, is the Beach Club on superb Newcastle Beach. It is a pleasant place to have lunch or dinner, or simply enjoy a cocktail. Those who prefer to be more active can rent windsurfing boards or snorkeling gear.

OUALIE BEACH HOTEL

Oualie Beach, Nevis, West Indies. Tel: (869) 469-9735 / Fax: (869) 469-9176

This lovely small hotel, built in typical Caribbean style architecture, is located on a superb beach.

It is made up of bungalows, each with a private terrace overlooking the sea – just a few yards away from the beach across a lush garden. New units are soon to be completed.

The kitchenette, bathroom and other facilities are so cozy that guests really feel at home in their bungalows.

The restaurant offers Continental-style and Carribean meals by prize-winning Chef, Patrick Fobert, served on a shaded terrace or on the veranda, according to the guests' wishes.

One could spend the entire day wading in the beautiful turquoise water. However, beach activities include scuba diving lessons, snorkeling, fishing and boating. The hotel maintains its own dive shop and equipment. An annual Fishing Tournament in October draws sport-fishing enthusiasts from all over the Caribbean.

Private cottages in the Caribbean style

Water sports are king at Oualie Beach

PINNEY'S BEACH HOTEL

P.O. Box 61, Charlestown, Nevis, West Indies. Tel: (869) 469-5207 / Fax: (869) 469-1088

Built on the island's most beautiful beach, within easy walking distance of Charlestown, the hotel offers a choice of rooms with balconies or cottages with a private patio. Both facilities are modern and comfortable, and afford an exceptional view of St. Kitts.

Enjoying the sun, or relaxing while sipping a cocktail by the swimming pool, are pleasures not to be overlooked.

In the evening, enjoy Continental and American meals, as well as local seafood specialities. Groups are cordially invited for evening events. An air-conditioned conference room adjoins the hotel.

Located at the water's edge, the hotel can organize any nautical activity offered on the island. Tennis courts are also available.

THE INN AT CADES BAY

Cades Bay, Nevis, West Indies. Tel: (869) 469-8139 / Fax: (869) 469-8129

The Inn offers 16 sea-front rooms with private verandahs, *en suite* bathrooms and stunning views. Amenities include tea/coffee-making facilities, air-conditioning, large ceiling fans, Cable T.V. and king/double bed configuration.

Tequila Sheila's, on the beach, serves daily island specials including superb fresh seafood; Eddy's, in town, features Caribbean specialities and a renowned "Happy Hour" where locals and visitors meet and mix. The Upstairs Bar offers a self-service breakfast.

A freshwater pool is available for guests, as well as a private half-moon beach. Scuba, snorkeling, sailing, car rentals, island hopping, fine dining, golf and many more activities can be arranged upon arrival.

CLIFFDWELLERS

Jones Estate, Nevis, West Indies. Tel: (869) 469-8262 / Fax: (869) 469-8195

Cliffdwellers' setting is among the most dramatic in the West Indies. Perched on a hill at the edge of the sea, Cliffdwellers offers coastal views to the north and south. To the west, the sunset sky and the intense blue of the Caribbean frame the mountains and inlets at neighbouring St.Kitts. Mount Nevis rises majestically to the east.

Cliffdwellers is a small, luxury villa resort, which means that all accommodations are in fully appointed villas, offering the privacy and comfort of home, with the amenities, service and hospitality of an intimate luxury hotel.

Each villa at Cliffdwellers has a verandah with sweeping water views and a bright, airy living room with a traditional West Indian cathedral ceiling. Some also have their own landscaped courtyards and pools. All are luxuriously furnished and fully equipped.

The perfect spot for sunbathing and enjoying a refreshing saltwater swim is Cliffdwellers' one hundred foot long, seaside pool. It is a lovely stroll from here along the shore to the sandy beach, and the reefs off the headlands offer wonderful snorkeling. Within minutes of the hotel is an excellent selection of other beaches on both the Caribbean and Atlantic sides of the island.

A smooth and silent tramway takes diners to the Tamarind Restaurant, with stops at individual villas along the way, offering breathtaking views and a breathsaving ride to the top.

THE FOUR SEASONS RESORT

P.O. Box 565, Charlestown, Nevis, West Indies. Tel: (869) 469-1111 / Fax: (869) 469-1040. Reservations: 1-800-332-3442

Caribbean resorts tend to reflect the style of their host island. If it's an island with a large city, expect to find big brassy casino hotels with glittery nightclubs and lots of partying. On islands that are popular with mainstream tourism and tour groups, it's not unusual to find dozens of cookie cutter hotels crowded along a single stretch of beach. And, on many of those undiscovered isles it can be hard to find accommodations at all. How, then, to explain the exuberant luxury of the Four Seasons Resort on the quaint island of Nevis? How to explain the delightful dichotomy of a world-class resort that has managed to blend in so seamlessly with its surroundings?

Explanations won't help. No matter how thoroughly one has read the guide books or has done his holiday homework, the first-time guest at Four Seasons Nevis simply cannot anticipate the treasure he's about to discover. Certainly the American Automobile Association found it to be extraordinary, honouring the resort with the Caribbean's first and only Five-Diamond Award.

After landing on the sister island of St.Kitts, (although some guests do arrive directly to the smaller airport in Nevis) guests board a private launch for the short ride to Nevis. During this cruise they are treated to a panoramic sea preview as the Nevis shoreline comes into focus : The graceful sprawl of the resort fills the horizon, underscored by the long stretch of golden sand of Pinney's Beach, and accented by the cloud-shrouded Nevis Peak which dramatically dominates the background. It's a beautiful sight, a picture-perfect sight. But, as all well know, beauty alone is hollow if it lacks a philosophy to give it substance. And that's where the Four Seasons tradition takes over.

Hospitality has always been the key element to any Four Seasons experience, and here in the islands that signature hospitality takes on a particular charm. Guests experience a profound sense of well-being which comes not from a fawning kind of pampering; rather, as the result of thoughtful consideration as to what elements contribute to a thoroughly enjoyable vacation.

90

The pier where guests arrive from St Kitts.

Just steps to the beach

The bungalows

No detail has been overlooked. No matter what the guest hopes to experience – whether it be luxurious surroundings, or days filled with sports challenges, with fine dining, or even stretches of benign solitude – it's all there for the taking.

Guests are welcomed personally, greeted at the pier on arrival, and escorted to their rooms in one of the two-story, West Indian plantation-style cottages which stretch out along the beach. All upstairs accommodations have large balconies; ground-level rooms open onto flower-bordered lanais. And all have glorious views, whether of the sea, or of the mountain and golf course.

Breakfast on the veranda

92

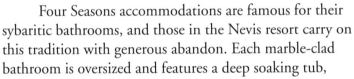

King-size bedroom . . .

Four Seasons accommodations are famous for their sybaritic bathrooms, and those in the Nevis resort carry on this tradition with generous abandon. Each marble-clad bathroom is oversized and features a deep soaking tub,

and bath.

separate shower, private toilet, and eight-foot marble counter with two vanities, and is stocked with all the deluxe amenities and stacks of fluffy towels one expects from a Four Seasons.

Guest room are spacious, with living and sleeping areas furnished in the island's signature mahogany pieces which reflect the traditional English designs brought over by the early settlers. Armoires, beds, chests and chairs in dark woods provide graceful counterpoint for the soft sensuous colours of the fabrics, the exotic tropical plants, and the shuttered doors that open to reveal the lush island setting.

The Presidential Suite

The Great House

The architectural style of the resort recalls a time in the islands in which high ceilings and upper-floor balconies were designed to capture and maximize the cooling breezes. Roofs peak sharply to points, and frilly gingerbread trim softens all the edges.

The Lobby

The resort's Great House is a charming example of this West Indian-style tradition. Here, guests gather in airy rooms, or in the cozy library with its club chairs and shelves of books, for a chat or for drinks before dinner. Or, they stroll along the veranda which overlooks the inviting free-form pool below and the ocean beyond.

The Nevis Yacht Club in the Library

The Dining Room

The Resort features three dining areas, the Grill Room, Dining Room and Cabana Restaurant located beach side. All restaurants feature international cuisine as well as an assortment of West Indian specialties.

The Grill Room

Pinney's Beach

Peter Burwash International Tennis Complex

Tennis buffs, too, discover a similar mix of sports challenge and serious pampering. The resort's tennis complex centers around 10 hard surface and clay courts, which are lighted for night play and managed by the world-renowned Peter Burwash International. There's also a stadium court for the weekly matches and tournaments which are arranged by the tennis pro. Nearby, there's a complete health club with fitness equipment, sauna, whirlpool, massage facilities and a beauty salon.

All this activity is just a short stroll from one of the most beautiful beaches in the Caribbean. A beach where, as you can imagine, guests don't just sunbathe on the sand; they recline on cushioned chaises that feature folding canvas hoods designed to screen both sun and wind. Beach attendants hover nearby to deliver drinks, as well as chilled towels and perhaps a refreshing spritz of chilled Evian water.

Too much relaxation? Four Seasons' beach is filled with equipment for all sorts of serious water sports, as well as a remarkable assortment of water toys for the kid in us all. Guests can opt for fishing, sailing or scuba, or can play in the surf aboard oversized water tricycles and see-through rafts.

It's a total vacation designed to please the senses, amuse the intellect, challenge the body, and soothe the soul. Guests leave the island of Nevis feeling closer to nature, infinitely relaxed, and better equipped to plunge back into the real world.

Total fitness

THE GOLF COURSE
Designed by Robert Trent Jones II

Sports-minded vacationers quickly realize they have come to the right place. The resort's golf course has been an island legend since the day it opened. Legendary not just because it's one of the few professional courses in the Caribbean. Nor is it legendary simply because it was designed by Robert Trent Jones II. It was his feat of turning an untenable terrain into a challenge, designing a course that hugs the side of the mountain. Outstanding among the many memorable features of this course is its 6,725 yard ascent up the volcanic slopes to the signature 15th hole which lies 420 feet above the sea with panoramic views that stretch all the way to St.Kitts and beyond. Golfers cover this mountain-climbing course in motorized carts, of course. And, because they are Four Seasons' guests, they can hail a passing beverage cart for some drinks, snacks and chilled towels.

The 11th hole

FOUR SEASONS RESORT ESTATES

P.O. Box 568, Charlestown, Nevis, West Indies. Tel: (869) 469-1199 Fax: / (869) 469-1971

Photography by Mary Nichols

Between Pinney's Beach and Mount Nevis, lie deep ravines and verdant rain forests. From cashew, mahogany and mango trees to hibiscus, poinciana and bougainvillea, an array of tropical flora abounds. Here, nestled in private enclaves amidst the spectacular Four Seasons golf course, are the luxurious estate homes and villas of Four Seasons Resort Estates.

Each home has been placed to take advantage of the magnificent diversity of scenery. The views are breathtaking, and the topography makes each site unique and every home an individual experience.

Photography by Joy von Tiedemann

Along the first fairway, you will find the villas of Palm Grove so wonderfully close to the Resort's facilities, from the Great House restaurants and shops to the pro shop and practice green. Just a few minutes by golf cart, you cross over the picturesque pond at the 8th tee and arrive at Sunset Hill Estates. Sunset Hill has it all; it's close to the Resort, yet private, and offers views of both Mount Nevis and the Caribbean, as well as the green vistas of the Robert Trent Jones II course. Nearby is Belmont Estates, a very secluded setting for a limited number of unique Estate Homes with extra-spacious gardens. Amidst "the back nine" on the site of an old coconut mill, almost 320 feet up the shoulders of Mount Nevis, are the Mahogany Hill Estate homes. Here, the villa owners enjoy a dazzling panorama of sea, immense blue skies, the fairways and Nevis Peak.

Everywhere, the highest standards of gracious living have been incorporated into this stylish Caribbean setting, with meticulously-crafted private residences reminiscent of the romantic style and grace of British West Indian plantation homes. Grand interiors open onto spacious covered galleries and landscaped private gardens. Touches of gingerbread, balustrades and louvered shutters reflect the island's heritage; and one of the island's oldest sugar mills blends into the distinctive landscape.

The Four Seasons care of the villas is comprehensive, 365 days of the year, The Resort ensures the villa is ready for the owners' arrival, and then carefully closes up on their departure. While in residence, it appears every owner's wish has been foreseen and any request is satisfied by a simple phone call. The flawless service for which Four Seasons is renowned is enjoyed to the maximum at Four Seasons Resort Estates.

Photography by Joy von Tiedemann

Photography by Joy von Tiedemann

MAP AND HOTEL LOCATOR

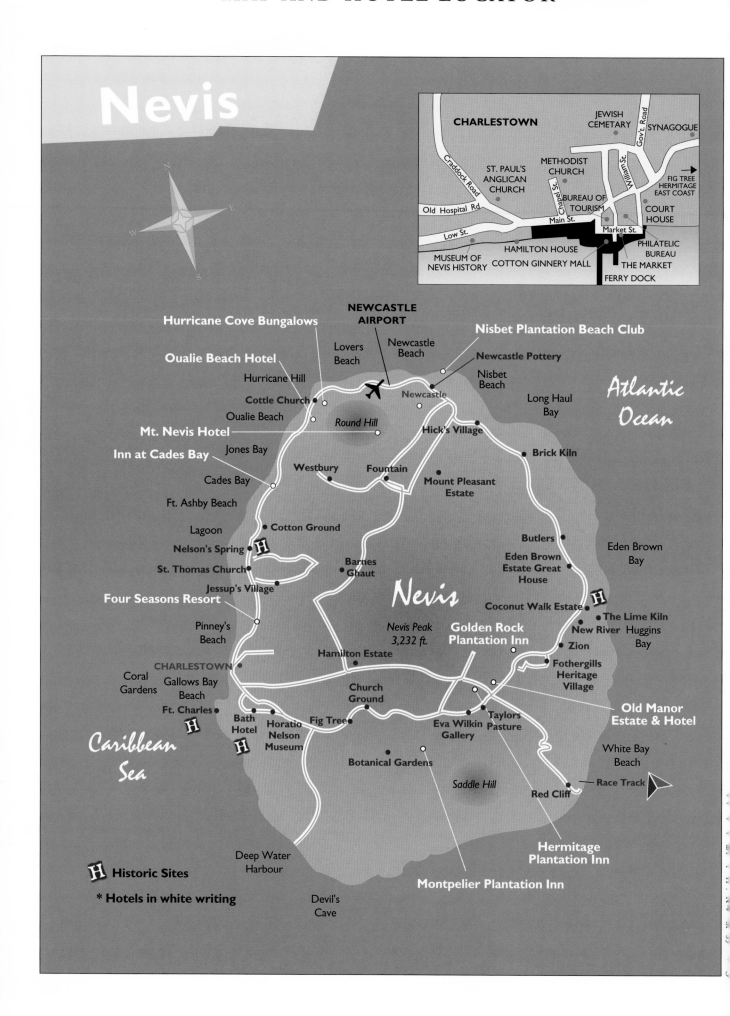

Nevis

CHARLESTOWN

JEWISH CEMETARY
SYNAGOGUE
Gov't. Road
St. Paul's Anglican Church
METHODIST CHURCH
William St.
FIG TREE HERMITAGE EAST COAST
Craddock Road
Chapel St.
Old Hospital Rd
BUREAU OF TOURISM
Main St.
Court House
Low St.
Market St.
PHILATELIC BUREAU
MUSEUM OF NEVIS HISTORY
HAMILTON HOUSE
COTTON GINNERY MALL
THE MARKET
FERRY DOCK

Hurricane Cove Bungalows
NEWCASTLE AIRPORT
Lovers Beach
Newcastle Beach
Nisbet Plantation Beach Club
Newcastle Pottery

Oualie Beach Hotel
Hurricane Hill
Newcastle
Nisbet Beach
Long Haul Bay
Atlantic Ocean

Cottle Church
Oualie Beach
Round Hill
Hick's Village
Brick Kiln

Mt. Nevis Hotel
Jones Bay
Westbury
Fountain
Mount Pleasant Estate

Inn at Cades Bay
Cades Bay
Ft. Ashby Beach

Lagoon
Cotton Ground
Butlers
Eden Brown Bay

Nelson's Spring
Barnes Ghaut
Eden Brown Estate Great House

St. Thomas Church
Nevis
Coconut Walk Estate
The Lime Kiln

Jessup's Village
New River
Huggins Bay

Four Seasons Resort
Zion

Pinney's Beach
Nevis Peak 3,232 ft.
Golden Rock Plantation Inn
Fothergills Heritage Village

CHARLESTOWN
Hamilton Estate

Coral Gardens
Gallows Bay Beach
Church Ground
Old Manor Estate & Hotel

Ft. Charles
Bath Hotel
Fig Tree
Eva Wilkin Gallery
Taylors Pasture
White Bay Beach

Caribbean Sea
Horatio Nelson Museum
Botanical Gardens
Saddle Hill
Race Track

Red Cliff

Hermitage Plantation Inn

Deep Water Harbour

H Historic Sites

Montpelier Plantation Inn

***** Hotels in white writing

Devil's Cave